MENTALLY TOUGH

MENTALLY TOUGH

THE PRINCIPLES OF WINNING AT SPORTS APPLIED TO WINNING IN BUSINESS

DR. JAMES E. LOEHR
and PETER J. McLAUGHLIN
with ED QUILLEN

M. EVANS AND COMPANY, INC.   NEW YORK

Library of Congress Cataloging-in-Publication Data

Loehr, James E.
  Mentally tough.

  Bibliography: p. 230
  1. Success in business. 2. Businessmen—Attitudes.
3. Businessmen—Health and hygiene. 4. Emotions.
I. McLaughlin, Peter J.   II. Quillen, Ed.
III. Title.
HF5386.L765   1986   650.1   86–19654

ISBN 0–87131–493–2

M. Evans and Company, Inc.
216 East 49 Street
New York, New York 10017

Design by Lauren Dong

Manufactured in the United States of America

9 8 7 6 5 4 3 2 1

Contents

To John, Peter, Jenny, and to Linda.
From the worst of times to the best of times.
Peter McLaughlin

To the many who have supported my work,
particularly during tough times.
Most importantly, my parents, Mary and Con.
James Loehr

"At the peak of tremendous and victorious effort . . . while the blood is pounding in your head, all suddenly becomes quiet within you. Everything seems clearer and brighter than before, as if great spotlights had been turned on. At that moment you have the conviction that you contain all the power in the world, that you have wings. There is no more precious moment in life than this, the white moment, and you will work very hard for years just to taste it again."

YURI VASILOV
Russian world-champion weight lifter

Foreword

A simple idea—if it is the right one—can change our lives. This book is based on a simple insight that can irrevocably change your life. The insight is this: it is not performance—getting off the seat of your pants to do the job—that will make you feel great; it is the state of feeling *great* that produces great performance.

Before you can do anything well, you must first feel well. For years we've had it backwards. "Just move yourself," the wise ones said, "and you'll feel better."

Wrong!

You must feel better in order to perform great. Feeling better is the result of an altered emotional state. It is the ability to change your emotional state that we call *mental toughness*. This book will give you that ability.

Mentally Tough has literally taken eleven years to write, from Dr. Loehr's original research on high level performance in sports to Mr. McLaughlin's work with business and management sales. Over the past six years, our team has woven together all the components of the Ideal Performance State, and researched and tested the strategies to get you there.

We began our workshops in Denver with members of the real estate profession and from there established our first Center for Peak Performance in Hilton Head, South Carolina. There we began to work with business executives from all over the country and from a variety of backgrounds: Cox Cable Corporation, AMF/Head, The Bell System and AT&T, to name a few.

The results were tremendously exciting. Executives, and in many cases their spouses, were able to start fine-tuning their emotions. They were beginning to relate the connection between feeling better and improving their performance state. We began an executive center at Sanibel Harbor. Here, Loehr's work in tennis had already attracted national acclaim.

Our workshops and speeches and the follow-up programs in the business arena have added more to our research base, and we have literally taken our ideas around the globe, from the United States to Japan, Canada and Europe.

Performance technology is a virgin field. New information comes in daily, we dissect it and add it to our training programs. This book weaves together all of our research and the practical information from our workshop and consulting experiences.

Most of the recent literature about the corporate world has concerned itself only with business and changes in business. This book, however, is about *you* and how you can train to do *more* than just cope. Coping is for beginners. Mental toughness if for winners.

1
PERFORMANCE BASICS

Some days, you are better.
You are quicker.
You are stronger.
You see more.
You accomplish more.
Solutions come to you.
You are on a roll.
You are better.

Why are you so much better on some days than on others? Is it only happenstance, a quirk of fate? Or is there some controllable way for you to perform consistently at the upper reaches of your abilities?

There is a way to be at your best whenever you want or need to be, and it is based upon your ability to control your emotions.

The quality of your performance reflects your emotional state as you perform. Your emotional state colors your perceptions of the external world, and it influences every activity of your body, from the speed of your heartbeat to the fluency of your speech.

From your own experience, you know how difficult it is to think clearly, especially about a complex subject, when you are enraged. You know how anxiety can keep you from relaxing so that you stay tense and don't get enough rest, which means you lack the energy you need to give your work the attention and quality it deserves, which makes you worried and anxious so you can't relax . . . And you know how depression can prevent you from caring about things you should care about.

Anger, anxiety, relaxation—these emotions and feelings change the chemistry of every cell in your body. When you are at your best, you are also in a specific emotional state, and you are chemically and physically different than at other times.

Despite what you may have been told, you can control your emotional state through simple and tested techniques. With this control, you will be able to put yourself in the proper emotional state to meet the challenges before you with the best that you have to offer. We call this ability mental toughness. It is neither a gift of heredity nor a stroke of luck; it is the result of applying strategies which can be learned and developed.

Some of these strategies may be new to you; others you already use every day. Any number of books describe top performance in minute detail. Many focus on one strategy to the exclusion of others and place the emphasis on immediate technique rather than fulfilling personal goals. This book is practical. It will show you how to recognize your emotional states and *use* strategies, alone or in combination, so that you can be at your best whenever you need to be.

THE DISCOVERY

Our work began in sports psychology, a relatively new branch of the discipline. As every fan knows, an athlete's performance varies widely from day to day. Top quarterbacks like John Elway or Joe Montana, who can't miss this week, threw eight interceptions last week. Yesterday's four-for-four hitter swings at pitches in the dirt today. John McEnroe's overpowering serves on Sunday smashed into the net on Saturday.

When we began our study, there was no good external explanation for this variation. The athletes brought essentially the same skills, practice, conditioning, coaching, and equipment to each contest. So we began to look for internal factors, and it was there that we discovered the constellation of feelings and attitudes we would call the Ideal Performance State. When the athletes experienced those feelings and attitudes, they performed at the upper limits of their abilities. When they performed in other emotional states, there was a gap between their potential and their performance.

In the fall of 1977, we began to systematically interview hundreds of athletes at all levels, from junior-high-schoolers to professionals. We wanted to discover the essence of what we would later call the Ideal Performance State. We were determined to find out what was really going on when athletes used terms like "pumped up," "treed," "psyched," "energized," "juiced," "wired," or "playing over my head."

Here's a composite of their descriptions:[1]

"I felt physically very relaxed, but really energized and pumped up. I experienced virtually no anxiety or fear, and the whole event was totally enjoyable. I felt a real sense of calmness and quiet inside, and everything just seemed to flow automatically. I really didn't have to think about what I was supposed to do; it just seemed to happen naturally.

"Even though I was really hustling, it seemed effortless. I always seemed to have enough time and energy and rarely felt rushed—at times, it was like slow motion. I felt as though I could do anything, as if I were in complete control. I was confident and positive.

"It also seemed easy to concentrate. I was totally tuned in to what I was doing. I was also super-aware—aware of everything but distracted by nothing. It almost seemed that I knew what was going to happen before it occurred."

Arnold Palmer has explained that golf at his best "involves a tautness of mind but not a tension of body. It has various manifestations. One is the concentration on the shot at hand. The other is the heightened sense of performance and renewal that endures through an entire round or an entire tournament. There is something spiritual, almost spectral, about the latter experience. You're involved in the action and vaguely aware of it, but your focus is not on the commotion but on the opportunity ahead. I'd liken it to a sense of reverie—not a dreamlike state but the somehow insulated state that a great musician achieves in a great performance. He's aware of what he is and what he's doing, but his mind is on the playing of his instrument with an internal sense of *rightness*—it is not merely mechanical, it is not only spiritual; it is something of both, on a different plane and a more remote one."[2]

Babe Ruth, recalling the time that he hit a home run after taking two strikes in the 1932 World Series, said: "Root threw me a fast ball. If I had let it go, it would have been called a strike. But this was *it*. I swung from the ground with everything I had and as I hit the ball every muscle in my system, every sense I had, told me that I had never hit a better one, that as long as I lived nothing would ever feel as good as this."[3]

WHITE MOMENTS

The Ideal Performance State—joy, confidence, and power—can be part of any human endeavor.

H. L. Mencken, the influential editor and literary critic, describing a writer's best times: "On his good days, for some reason quite incomprehensible to him, all the processes and operations of his mind take on an amazing slickness. Almost without conscious effort he solves technical problems that have badgered him for weeks."[4]

U.S. Representative Barbara Boxer of California: "It's like being on a roll. I am able to accomplish a great deal with a minimum of effort. My energy keeps building and gets transferred to whomever I am working with."[5]

Captain Charles Congrad, Jr. of the *Apollo* moon expedition said of his lunar landing: "It's just like old-home week. I feel like I've been here many times before."[6]

Tom Simpson, president of Norwegian Caribbean Lines:

"I seem to be able to stay relaxed in what would ordinarily be very tense meetings. I feel as if I am not trying as hard as usual and yet I am much more effective."[7]

Hans Eysenck, noted and controversial psychologist: "I often feel—and it's a funny feeling—you might have a very ordinary car and put an eighteen-cylinder engine into it from an aeroplane. . . . which dictates my books and tells me what to do in the way of research. I am almost possessed by it."[8]

The Ideal Performance State is like any other deep-felt human experience—it has the same emotional components, regardless of the nature of the performance. Just as the elation of victory is the same for the attorney who has just heard a favorable verdict as it is for the pitcher who hurls the last out to win the World Series, so too is the Ideal Performance State always the same, regardless of the circumstances. We went from junior-high-school janitors to corporate presidents, and we heard the same state being described. For instance, a diesel mechanic described his finest hour this way: "Every now and then, there's a day when I get about six times as much done, because I do everything right the first time and so I never have to do anything over. The tools are always where they're supposed to be; it's almost like they jump into my hand. And even if it's a rush job where they want it yesterday, it seems like I've got all the time in the world."[9]

If you still believe that performance is something other people have to do, it is time you got out of the bleachers and into the arena. Every economist who has bothered to predict the future of American careers sees the same trends emerging: more innovation, more creativity, better products, changing structures, growing competition, constant challenge—in short, demands that must be met by performing at the upper reaches of your abilities. No matter what you do, you must think of yourself as a performer if you are to meet the inevitable challenges of a changing world.[10]

EMOTIONS AND PERFORMANCE

The Ideal Performance State is part of the human heritage, and everyone experiences it from time to time.[11] It is characterized by strong positive emotions. When people feel good, they perform at their best. When the emotional climate is wrong, performance suffers.

The relationship between your emotional state and your performance goes like this:

1. Your level of performance is a direct reflection of the way you feel inside: When you feel good, you perform well.
2. Performing at the best of your abilities at any given moment occurs without conscious deliberation when the right internal conditions have been established.
3. To achieve mental toughness, you must develop the ability to create and maintain positive internal feelings regardless of the circumstances.

Which comes first, though—the positive feelings, or the outstanding performance? Is the Ideal Performance State the result of good performance, or is it the cause of good performance?

If you think feeling good is a result of doing well, you've got it backward. Thanks to the configuration of the human nervous system, the emotions have to be in place first.

Central Control

In order to understand why emotional states seem to dictate performance levels, we have to look to the sciences of neurophysiology and biochemistry.

To understand the basics of the human nervous system, it is important to realize that nerve cells are not wired together like a string of Christmas tree lights. The cells do not touch; instead, there is a tiny gap between them called a synapse. Various chemicals, known as neurotransmitters, carry the impulses across the synapses between cells.[12]

Similar chemicals, called hormones, are carried through the bloodstream; when they reach the proper gland or nervous center, these chemicals cause a response. At any given time, then, the state of your central nervous system—your brain and its major connections to the network of nerves to all parts of your body—is a matter of chemistry. One powerful chemical in your nervous system is norepinephrine, which is released when you are alarmed. In normal quantities, norepinephrine (both a hormone and a neurotransmitter) produces an energized, alert state. If you continue to be alarmed, however, then the norepinephrine makes you edgy and anxious. Another neurotransmitter, serotonin, causes feelings of relaxation and comfort.[13]

Some signals carried by the nervous system are voluntary. Moving your hand can be a conscious, deliberate act. Others are reflexive: If your hand touches something hot, you will jerk it back before the pain even registers in the conscious regions of your brain. The reflex action was handled by a different part of the central nervous system.

In the core of the brain, atop the spinal cord, is a wishbone-shaped collection of glands and processing centers known collectively as the limbic system. We will be referring to it often, because it is the seat of human emotion. For example, if you are energized, there will be more norepinephrine than usual in your limbic system, and this leads to rapid physical changes, such as dilated pupils (making your eyes more sensitive, so that you are more aware of your surroundings) and accelerated pulse (bringing more blood to the muscles, so that you have more energy for a response).

Your emotional state, and thus much of your mental and physical ability to perform, is a reflection of the balance of neurotransmitters in your limbic system.

Besides controlling emotion, the limbic system functions as something of a central switchboard. Messages from other parts of the body to the brain go through the limbic system, and when the brain responds, again the impulse goes through the limbic system. If you make a conscious decision to raise your hand and scratch your ear, the conscious decision is made in the frontal lobes of the brain. The impulses go through the limbic system to the cerebellum at the back of the brain, which controls many muscular actions. The cerebellum sends an impulse—again passing through the limbic system—to the nerves in your hand. And the signals from your hand, such as the announcement that the ear has been reached, go through the limbic system before they are registered in your consciousness.[14]

Your emotional state and the chemical balance within your limbic system are merely two ways of looking at the same phenomenon. Emotional chemistry affects perception and the transmission of thoughts and actions—and what else is performance?

Here's a simple example of the relationship. If you are relaxed, you find it easy to hold your hand before you and keep it steady. But if you are tense, it does not matter how much you *want* your hand to be steady; it will still quiver. In fact, the more you consciously want that hand to quit shaking, the more the hand will vibrate. The only way to stop it from shaking is to relax—to change your emotional state. This changes the chemistry of the central nervous system, which in turn allows those taut hand muscles to relax.

Your emotional state determined whether you could perform a very simple act: holding your hand steady. Consider the delicate balance of mind and muscle required to speak, write, adjust, gesture, or drive, and you see how your emotional state can have such a dramatic effect on your ability to perform.

The critical understanding which many performers miss is that they are physically and chemically different when they change emotional states. Emotional states are not something extraneous; they are at the core of your perceptions and responses. When you go from happiness to anger, from nervousness to calm, or from boredom to excitement, you change your biochemistry. You change your alertness to what is going on around you, you change your perception of those events, you change your responses to your perceptions. When you change your emotional state, you change your ability to perform. With the right emotional climate, you perform at your best.

A good example of this lies in an analysis of the Reagan–Mondale debates in 1984. In the first debate, Reagan's aides reported that he seemed nervous and anxious, not in his usual state of good humor. We who watched on television could see that his performance was below par; 54 percent of those polled thought Mondale had done the better job. For the second debate, Reagan reported feeling relaxed, calm, eager, and spontaneous.[15] It showed; his performance was exceptional. His feelings and emotions led to changes in his biochemistry which were reflected in a superlative performance before millions of Americans.

Bridging the Gap

The right internal climate helps to bridge a gap, the gap between what you might do and what you actually do, the gap between your potential and realizing that potential. Attempting to perform well with the wrong internal climate is like trying to get a seed (which is nothing more than potential) to grow in frozen soil—nothing happens.

But as soon as the climate improves, with warmth and moisture and nutrients, then the seed can begin to draw from the soil and grow. Establishing the right internal climate has the same effect on potential performance as the changing of the seasons has on potential plants.

INSIDE THE IDEAL PERFORMANCE STATE

During our analysis of more than four hundred descriptions by performers of their finest hours, we consistently encountered twelve distinct categories of feelings. During a top performance, these feelings always manifested themselves in one way or another. To the extent that these feelings were not present, the performance level invariably suffered.

Much of what we have learned about these feelings and their intimate connection to top-level performance flies in the face of common wisdom. Certain prevalent myths encourage people to think in ways that almost guarantee poor performance. "Trying harder," for instance—could you make your tensed hand stop quivering by "trying harder"? The answer there lies in the calmer state of "trying softer."

The constellation of feelings that form the Ideal Performance State is not a common experience—and neither is winning. When thirty-two people enter a tournament, only one will win. Of the twenty-eight teams in the NFL, only one takes the Super Bowl trophy. There's only one CEO in any corporation. Of the thirty-five thousand MBAs minted every year, only a handful will ever lead a company in the Fortune 500.

Common emotional reactions lead to common performance. Winning is an uncommon result.

UNDERSTANDING PEAK PERFORMANCE FEELINGS

This uncommon collection of emotions, described by the performers we interviewed, deserves to be examined in detail.[16]

Mental Calmness

There is a characteristic inner stillness associated with every great performance. Many people try to meet a challenge by psyching themselves up into a fast, accelerated mental state. This is not the state of great performance. During the white moments, there is a very real sense of internal calm and quiet—almost a sense of performing in slow motion.

Physical Relaxation

The physical state is a reflection of the mental state, and vice versa. Physical tenseness ruins performance, whether you're trying to hit a tennis ball or you're delivering a speech. During your finest hours, the muscles are relaxed, not taut.

Freedom From Anxiety

Myth has it that some anxiety helps; it motivates you, perhaps. But in our Ideal Performance State research, it became clear that anxiety militates against excellence. Anxiety leads to physical and mental tension and provokes an undesirable shift in focus from the performance itself to its outcome or possible repercussions. There is an exception: If you feel flat and just can't get going, anxiety will provide a source of energy. Sometimes any performance is better than none at all. But anxiety is negative energy, and no performance fueled by anxiety will be as good as one fueled from a positive source.

Energy

This is the single most important ingredient of the twelve, and the most misunderstood. It is the energy that comes when you are loose, calm, and free of anxiety. Every top performance is propelled by a seemingly boundless supply of mental and physical energy, drawn from the positive emotions. Athletes describe it as being "pumped up," "jazzed," "psyched," "revved," or "wired." It is energy without tension.

Optimism

The optimism during top performances comes from a strong belief that whatever the challenge, the performer will find a way to meet it. Top performers never run out of options, and their optimism reflects this knowledge.

Twenty-five years of biofeedback research confirm that negative feelings, attitudes, and emotions impact the physiology in dramatically different ways than positive emotions do.

Enjoyment

The principle is simple: When you find joy in it, you perform it well. When it ceases to be fun, performance suffers. If you believe that you enjoyed it because you did it well, then you've got it backward. You did it well because you enjoyed it, because you were having fun as you performed. This state of fun is all-important to good performance; it represents a limitless source of positive energy.

Effortlessness

When your mind and body are working in harmony, even though you're giving your all to the task, it almost seems easy. When the biochemistry is right, achieving great goals and overcoming major obstacles seem nearly effortless.

Automaticity

During great performances, the action is automatic, almost intuitive or instinctive. The right responses come naturally, without hesitation or deliberation. Performers often refer to the "paralysis by analysis syndrome." They begin to focus on the mechanics, and as they concentrate on one part of their performance, the rest suffers. During a performance, instinct is always more effective than conscious, deliberate thought.

Alertness

Finest hours always include an extraordinary awareness and a heightened sense of self. Athletes know the positions of their bodies and of the players around them; they perceive who is likely to do what. An executive will sense accurately the pulse of the surroundings, but simultaneously stay riveted to the task at hand. This alertness almost seems like mind-reading because the responses are so quick and appropriate. But it isn't ESP; when you are this alert, you notice signals that are always present but usually unperceived—a twitch of the lip or a flick of an eyebrow that indicates the other person's response.

Focus

The importance of concentration is no surprise; it is essential to any good performance to be able to focus on a specific target and resist distraction. However, the focus of top performance does not result from conscious effort at concentration; instead, it is a product of the mixture of calmness and positive energy that characterizes the Ideal Performance State. In this state, the focus is on the performance itself, not on the score, standings, profits, or possible repercussions.

Self-confidence

The self-confidence of the Ideal Performance State is nothing more than the strong internal belief that one can meet the challenges. This provides calm when the circumstances might otherwise evoke panic, anxiety, anger, or tension.

Control

This is simply the feeling that you are in control of yourself and your responses to events. You are not a passive victim of circumstance. You cannot always control events, but you can control your emotional responses.

GETTING THERE

The Ideal Performance State parallels your most delightful sexual moments. This is no accident—at those times, you are physically relaxed, mentally calm, free from anxiety, full of energy, responding intuitively, and delighting in every second.

No matter what the performance—the sheer physical strength demanded of a weight lifter, the dexterity of a surgeon, the mental gymnastics of a scientist, the applied insight of an executive—the Ideal Performance State includes the same constellation of feelings. Since the Ideal Performance State results from that emotional and biochemical balance, the key to top performance in any endeavor is getting into the right emotional state.

Tradition has it that emotions are like the wind: They cannot be controlled, but they can be channeled into useful energy under favorable conditions.

The reality is that you are not doomed to poor performance on those days when your emotional balance is tilted. You can learn to exert significant control over your emotional balance.

THE TWO-WAY STREET

Emotions manifest themselves physically. Anxiety brings tense muscles and cold sweat. Fear intensifies those responses. Confidence engenders regular deep breaths. Hunger leads to distraction and the inability to focus.

But it works both ways. Your physical actions and conscious thoughts, if directed properly, can control your emotions.[17] With that control, you can perform at the upper reaches of your abilities, regardless of external circumstances.

To make this clear, let's look at the traditional concept of top performance. That sequence goes something like this.

GOOD PERFORMANCE *leads to* → **POSITIVE EMOTIONAL STATE**

Our findings support a different paradigm.

POSITIVE EMOTIONAL STATE *leads to* → **GOOD PERFORMANCE**

Consistently achieving high levels of performance is nothing more or less than knowing how to maintain a special kind of emotional control. Once the proper emotions are in place, your genius—your brightness, quickness, talents, intelligence—will emerge.

HOW TO USE THIS BOOK

For you to attain the positive emotional state necessary for you to be at your best, we have developed a specific procedure.

1. Assess your current emotional state.
2. Implement a strategy to adjust your emotional state. This may be attitude, motivation, visualization, diet, breath control, exercise, humor, or ritual.
3. Feel positive, energizing emotions.
4. Perform at your best.

The next chapter explains how to assess your emotional state at any given time. With that knowledge, you can move from one state to another by using various strategies, which we explain in some detail in separate chapters. These strategies give you the ability to control your emotions so that you can always perform in the upper ranges of your skills and talents. And in the last two chapters, we demonstrate applications of the strategies, especially for stress management and creativity.

Learning to control your emotional balance is not an overnight process, although you will see immediate results as soon as you start to implement the strategies. But it will take time and experimentation to learn which strategies work best for you in which situations. For example, when should you visualize to relax, and when should you use breath control? In which situations should you energize yourself with exercise, and when would ritual work better? You are unique, and so is your biochemistry.

We recommend that you read through this book once, thoroughly, to establish the overall concept and see how your thoughts and actions can control your emotional state. Then go back, chapter by chapter, and practice each chapter's specific strategy until you are comfortable with it and know how it works for you. You will then have developed a repertoire of skills, so that no matter what the external circumstances, you will have at hand a way to control your emotional response.

NOT MAGIC

Controlling your emotions for top performance is not a form of magic. There are three factors that determine how well you perform: talent, practice, and attitude. Emotional control cannot replace talent or the skills developed through practice. But emotional control can give you the stamina required to practice and the staying power necessary for achieving your goals, along with the attitudes required for performing at the upper levels of your abilities.

Emotional control will insure that you are realizing your talents. It will allow you to consistently put forth the best that is within you, performing excellently in your chosen arena, no matter what that may be: tennis, software development, management, photography, accounting, law, woodworking . . . Mental toughness gives you the ability to summon your best whenever you want or need to.

Courage, Ernest Hemingway once said, is grace under pressure.[18] The world has no difficulty in providing the pressure; mental toughness provides the grace.

2
MAINTAINING POSITIVE ENERGY:
The Fuel of Mental Toughness

IDEAL PERFORMANCE STATE: MOOD CONTROL

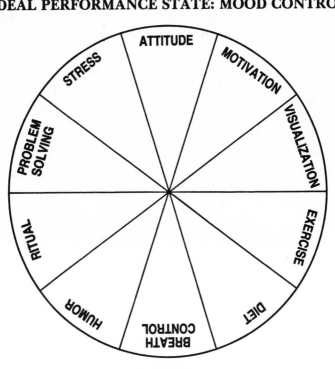

STRATEGIES

At any given time, you're in one of four Internal Energy States.

Learn to recognize those states, and you can move from one to another.

Moving to the proper Internal Energy State allows you to perform at your best.

On February 22, 1980, the world witnessed the power of positive energy. Some called it "momentum," others referred to "team spirit," and there were those who said it had to be "inspiration" or "luck" when the United States ice hockey team defeated the Soviet Union in the 1980 Winter Olympics.

By whatever name, it was real. You didn't have to be on the rink to sense the presence of something powerful; its effects were everywhere. Fear, anxiety, negativism, and self-doubt had been banished by Coach Herb Brooks and his "Boys of Winter"; they exuded confidence, determination, self-belief, and joy.

Judged by an objective standard—rating the teams man-for-man down the line-up in stick dexterity, skating form, body-checking skills, playing experience, etc.—the United States team should have been blown off the ice in the early rounds. Even Brooks thought so before the Olympics: "You know what our chances are? Slim and none."[1]

But instead of being eliminated, the United States upset Czechoslovakia 7–3 on February 14. Two days later, Norway went down 5–1. On February 18, it was Rumania's turn to succumb, 7–2; then West Germany, 4–2.

It was time to face a powerful Soviet squad. Coach Brooks gathered his team for some final words, and this time he didn't mention slim chances. "You're born to be hockey players, you're meant to be here. The moment is yours."[2]

It was their moment, and it wasn't destiny and it wasn't luck. The Americans skated onto the rink and out-performed the Russians, even though the Russian team possessed more experienced players with superior skills. Members of the United States team performed at the peak of their physical skills and talents; the Russians did not.

That made the difference. The intense positive energy of the U.S. hockey players put them into the Ideal Performance State. They were able to extract the utmost from what abilities they brought; the Russians played below their best.

The ability to summon a massive flow of intense positive energy when meeting a challenge—being mentally tough —brought victory to a team that could have won in no other manner.

KINDS OF ENERGY

You know when you're energized—pumped up and ready to go—and if you think for a moment, you'll recall that there are two very different ways to feel highly energized.

In one high-energy state, you're angry, perhaps raging. It's all you can do to keep from hitting or kicking something. Your face is flushed, your heart is pounding, your breathing is shallow and rapid, you are focused on the object of your anger and it's extremely difficult to think about anything else.[3]

In the other high-energy state, you're at your best. You're performing. Your pulse is speeded but not pounding, your breathing is deep and regular, you are focused on your performance but you're aware of everything around you. If you're not in the Ideal Performance State, you're certainly close to it.

There are also two ways that you can feel when you don't have energy. You can be relaxed and taking it easy, or depressed and withdrawn. In neither case do you feel like doing much, but the two states feel very different from each other. In one you're relaxed; in the other, you're not.

Your energy state is thus characterized by two factors: how pleasant or unpleasant you feel, and how intensely you feel the urge to do something. Given that, we can make a chart to illustrate the four Internal Energy States and their relationships.

INTERNAL ENERGY STATES
AND ASSOCIATED EMOTIONS

High Intensity

HIGH POSITIVE	HIGH NEGATIVE
Energy without tension	*Tension with energy*
Energetic	Fearful
Lively	Anxious
Stimulated	Angry
Vigorous	Frustrated
Enthusiastic	Upset
Cooperative	Vengeful

Pleasant ————————————————————— **Unpleasant**

LOW POSITIVE	LOW NEGATIVE
Neither energy nor tension	*Tension without energy*
Relaxed	Bored
Sleepy	Uninterested
Weary	Annoyed
Little desire	Irritated
Out of gas	Burned out
Low motivation	

Low Intensity

CHANGING STATES

Your feelings—your emotional state—determine how well you perform. Doing well is the result of feeling good. Being mentally tough means being able to control your emotional state so that when a challenge comes, you can quickly shift into the High Positive Internal Energy State to meet it. And when you're not facing a challenge, when it's time to relax and recharge, you will know how to stay on the positive side, in the Low Positive, rather than succumbing to inertia or depression.

In short, we are talking about the ability to change Internal Energy States at will, using any of several strategies, or a combination of the strategies explained in this book.

To get anywhere, you have to know where you're starting. The first step is to become intimately familiar with the Internal Energy States so that you always know which one you're in; with that knowledge you can deploy strategies to move you into the High Positive for performance and the Low Positive for relaxation.

The Low Positive

This is not an unpleasant state. It's the way you should feel when you're relaxing. You're calm and easygoing, receptive but not very attentive to what's going on around you.

It's not a performance state, but it's the place to be if you're just going through a routine that does not demand great intensity. You daydream and your mind wanders.

When confronted with a potentially stressful situation while in the Low Positive, you try to ignore it, perhaps hoping it will go away or that someone else will take care of it. If you do get involved, the involvement is tentative and half-hearted; you're not into it. Your performance will reflect this.

The Low Negative

Nothing seems to interest you; what does catch your attention always seems to annoy, irk, peeve, or irritate. This is where you perform at your absolute worst. You keep asking yourself why God goes to so much trouble to make you miserable. You feel drained and listless and depressed and overwhelmed; you'd like to hide somewhere.

Every normal person experiences this state in varying degrees. In its mildest form, the Low Negative might result from something minor—say the cancellation of a meeting you were looking forward to. The Low Negative might deepen if you don't get a promotion you believed you had coming; the loss of employment often propels people into the Low Negative. Illness, such as a bad case of flu, can put you into the Low Negative. A deep Low Negative is the usual state of grief at the loss of a loved one.

When a challenge appears and you're in the Low Negative, the last thing you want to do is perform. This is perfectly understandable, because you're in no condition to perform; anything you do will be marred unless you can get out of the Low Negative before you perform.[4]

The High Negative

You're ready to fight anything that gets in your way, and you're on your way to getting even with whatever angers you. This is the well-known adrenaline-rush "fight or flight" reaction.[5]

You're boiling with energy, but it goes everywhere. The batter in the High Negative swings, with megaton force, at pitches in the dirt. In the office, you call someone you have to reach, and you get a busy signal; you slam the phone into the receiver, and then shout at the next person who asks you something.

This state evolved as a method of dealing with saber-toothed tigers and similar menaces. The blood has been pulled from the digestive system and the fine muscles to energize the big muscles so that you can run fast to get away from the threatening tiger, or swing a club hard.[6]

For thousands of years, this was an appropriate response to the challenges that humans faced. On occasion, it still is. But it extracts a tremendous cost. In the High Negative, you sacrifice future well-being for immediate strength. Those who spend much time in the High Negative—the classic Type As who are always in a hurry, who get angered any time something doesn't go their way—are three times as likely to die of a heart attack, and they succumb at early ages to ulcers, hypertension, and other by-products of stress.[7]

There are times when the High Negative might still be an appropriate response. In a genuine life-threatening situation, the High Negative often makes the difference; it allows you to exchange the certainty of immediate demise for the likelihood of a shorter life expectancy.

But people who don't know how to control their Internal Energy States often find themselves provoked into the High Negative by situations that are not even close to being immediate mortal dangers—events like not being able to find a parking place, getting stuck in traffic, losing something in a filing cabinet, being told "I'm sure I put that check in the mail."

In the High Negative, you perform better than in either of the low states; any energy is better than none. But it comes at a fearful price, and the performance will never be as good as in the High Positive.

The High Positive

It means energy without tension, and joy in the performance itself. You're focused and aware, full of enthusiasm but in control.

The High Positive sounds like the Ideal Performance State, but they're not quite the same thing. The Ideal Performance State is the "white moment" when every part of your body and brain is functioning perfectly.

The quality of your performance is influenced by many factors—what you ate, your breathing, your mental imagery, the performance environment, the time of day—and every one must be perfectly attuned for you to achieve the "white moment": you at your best. Some of those factors are beyond your control; they are matters of happenstance.

The High Positive represents you at the best level you can consistently maintain. And the High Positive is the gateway to the Ideal Performance State. Everyone gets into the Ideal Performance State through the High Positive. Being in the High Positive is not a guarantee that you'll enter the Ideal Performance State, but the High Positive is your consistent best. You'll shine more brilliantly at some times than at others, but you'll always shine brightly in the High Positive.

To put it another way, in the Ideal Performance State, 100 percent of your potential is being realized during the performance. It's you at your absolute best. In the High Positive, it's 85 to 90 percent; in the High Negative, 60 percent; 25 percent in the Low Positive; and 10 percent in the Low Negative.

FOCUS ON THE CONTROLLABLE

The Ideal Performance State depends on factors you cannot always control; you can control whether you are in the High Positive.

The idea is to focus on what you can control. Get into the High Positive when it's time to perform or when a challenge appears. If you end up in the Ideal Performance State, so much the better, but by getting into the High Positive, you've done everything you can willfully do to muster your skills and talents to meet the challenge.

Focusing on the controllable works in another way. You generally cannot control events, nor can you control what other people do. But you can control your Internal Energy State, which in turn controls your response. And generally, it is not events in themselves that give you trouble and induce stress, but your responses to events.

Consider a mundane workday annoyance. The day starts routinely enough; you're ready to leave for work. Upon reaching your car, you find a flat tire. You remember that you lent your spare to a friend last week, who hasn't gotten around to returning it.

Your Internal Energy State, not the event itself, will determine whether the situation is stressful.

Low Negative: You think about calling your employer and announcing that you're taking the day off. But the

more you try to think of a plausible excuse, the harder it gets. The thought of even dialing the phone becomes worrisome
—suppose the wrong person answers? You lean on your car for a while; that's about all either of you is good for. Maybe your company planned to file for Chapter 11 today anyway. It figures. You go back inside; eventually you call in, mumbling so much that you're sure they think you've got the grandfather of all head colds.

High Negative: You tell yourself that it's about time you changed your mind about the National Rifle Association. You really should keep a .357 magnum around the house for these emergencies. Or maybe some dynamite. Who needs friends anyway, especially a freeloading lowlife who deliberately and maliciously lied to you about when he'd return your tire? You try to call the tire-borrower, can't reach him, and slam the phone down. Eventually you catch a ride to work, but the entire day is annoyance piled upon frustration thrown upon rage. Everyone at the first meeting seems to babble and babble, without ever getting close to the point; you want to tell them all to shut up and quit bothering you with such irrelevant drivel.

Low Positive: Maybe you should walk to work. Nice day for that, kind of. But it rained last night and there might be puddles. You're wearing the wrong shoes for that, and you can't remember what you did with the right ones. Which footwear would be right for this, anyway? Funny how they never show that in the ads, isn't it? But having dry feet really is important. One of life's great pleasures, and we take it for granted most of the time. There must be other things like that, and if you think for a while you'll come up with dozens, but it's so hard to stay focused. You almost don't notice a neighbor honking and offering you a ride to work—where you don't get much done anyway. The first meeting is only slightly less boring than watching paint dry, and it is all you can do to keep from yawning.

High Positive: Didn't you read somewhere about a novel concept? Instead of calling in sick, people could call in well, and take a day off to enjoy good health? You smile at the prospect, but realize it's imprudent today; you've got a meeting at 10 A.M. It's a gorgeous day and it's only four miles. You call in and explain that there are two options: They can promote you and send a company limo for you, or you're going to be somewhat late because you're walking to work. During the walk, you go over strategies for the meeting; you arrive relaxed yet enthusiastic, and the meeting goes well. That night your friend comes by with the tire, an apology, and some wine.

THE SAME FLAT TIRE

It was the same flat tire and the same missing spare in each scenario. If, as is traditionally believed, the situation determined the response, then you'd have responded identically, no matter how you felt.

But it doesn't work that way. It generally isn't the situation that makes the difference, but how you respond to the situation. It isn't events that cause stress, but how you respond to events. How you respond is a function of your Internal Energy State—your emotions.

It makes the difference between getting somewhere and staying on the treadmill.

One school of business studied 400 executives who had made it to the top, and compared them to 400 who fell by the wayside during their careers. The idea was to discover how those who made it differed from those who didn't.[8]

Education was not the key factor, because high-school dropouts were running companies while Harvard MBAs were falling into dead ends. Experience? Then those at the top should have been older; that wasn't the case. Technical skills, social skills, and dozens of other career-related variables were examined as well, and those factors didn't provide the explanation, either.

The only single quality which distinguished those who made it from the also-rans was the way in which they handled stress. The researchers found that successful executives looked upon stressful situations as challenges—problems to solve and overcome. The also-rans looked upon stressful situations as, well, stress. Something to be avoided because everybody knows that stress is deadly. Or something to be obliterated by force of will, if not just simply force.

THE WRONG STUFF

When you are faced with a crisis, the typical reaction takes one of three forms:

Tanking: In sports, "tanking" is throwing in the towel before it's over. You go through the motions without investing yourself in what you're doing. You feel ambivalent, uncommitted. Your energy level stays at the Low Positive. By approaching a situation in this way, you protect your ego: "I could have done it if I had really tried." And since you didn't really try, it's no reflection on your skills and talents that you failed. Remember that a half-hearted effort may produce plausible excuses, but it virtually guarantees failure.

The first key to avoiding this problem is commitment. Don't get involved in projects that you're not committed to, and once you're in, perform with all the strength you can summon. Second, don't be afraid to fail. Failure is part of the price of success, and some failures are inevitable.

Temper: Another simple way to deal with crisis or conflict is to lose your temper. Something irks you and you become enraged. You jump into the High Negative, anywhere from a slow simmering anger to a full eruptive boil. This is merely another way to avoid commitment—you can blame whatever set you off: "Boy, I just lost my temper

when they said that about our products." And that keeps
you from having to deal with the problem. Variations include becoming hypercritical, cynical, or accusatory, or
presenting a dismal mood to the world. Actually, all are
tanks—ways to withdraw from, rather than respond to,
the challenge.

Choking: Athletes talk about choking all the time.
Choking is fear—fear that you won't make it, fear that you
don't have what it takes. It's another aspect of the High
Negative, accompanied by accelerated heart rate, more
muscle tension, shallow respiration, and concentration on
the consequences instead of the task: "If I don't do this
right, I'll lose my promotion" or "I'll be humiliated if this
doesn't turn out."

Athletes hold no monopoly on choking; it happens to
executives, secretaries, and cabdrivers. The response is so
ingrained in the human nervous system that it can never
be eliminated. No matter how controlled you are, the possibility of choking always remains. But the better you can
control your Internal Energy States, the less often you'll
choke and the shorter each incident will be.

You will not learn to deal with the choke if you allow
yourself the options of tanking or temper. Mastering fear
requires full commitment—risking 100 percent of your
effort and energy.

Withdrawing does reduce the nervous fear that causes
choking—but with the result of mediocre performance.
Only performers choke; the audience doesn't, and neither
do the benchwarmers. Choking is one of the risks of being
in a position that matters.

One thing we stress in our workshops is that *it is better
to choke than to tank because choking means you're still in it.
You're fighting. You still care. You're taking a risk.* The first
step is to quit withdrawing. When you stop tanking, you
start choking. When you've mastered the strategies of Internal Energy State control, you'll be able to stop the choke
before it affects your performance.

TO TANK: In the face of problems you withdraw energy and commitment (find excuses for not trying).

TO BECOME ANGRY: In the face of problems you allow your energy to turn negative (angry, upset, temper).

TO CHOKE: In the face of problems, you become nervous or afraid. (This is actually a sign of real progress.)

TO BECOME CHALLENGED: The key to being mentally tough! In the face of problems, you find yourself investing more positive energy. You have come to LOVE solving problems!

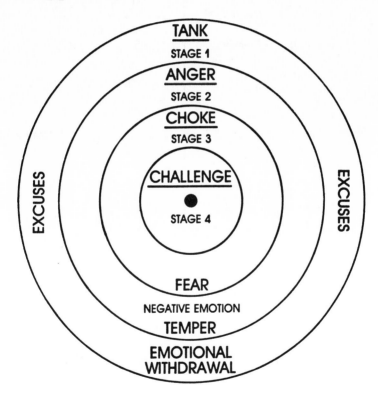

STAGE 1—Low Energy
STAGE 2—Negative Energy (Anger)
STAGE 3—Negative Energy (Fear)
STAGE 4—Focused High Positive Energy

How you respond to an event almost always has more to do with how you feel—your Internal Energy State—than with the nature of the event. Depending on your emotional climate, your response typically takes one of the forms outlined in the following chart.

INTERNAL ENERGY STATES
AND RESPONSE TO STRESS AND CRISIS

High Intensity

HIGH POSITIVE
Energy without tension
 	
The Challenge Response:
  Find a way to make it,
  and if that doesn't
  work, there's always
  another way.
	HIGH NEGATIVE
	Tension with energy
	
	The Temper Tank
	  Response
	The Choke Response

Pleasant	**Unpleasant**

LOW POSITIVE
Neither energy nor tension
 	
The Avoidance Response:
  Maybe it'll go away.
 	
The Half-Hearted
Response:
  That way, there's
  always an excuse.
	LOW NEGATIVE
	Tension without energy
	
	The Withdrawal Tank
	  Response:
	  I'm overwhelmed, I
	  can't handle this.

Low Intensity

PICKING YOUR CHALLENGES

What separates mental toughness from "workaholism"? What's the difference between the commitment to top performance and the compulsive overcommitment that destroys private life, family life, and sometimes sanity itself?

The major difference is picking your challenges and, once engaged, being committed to mastering them.

One of the most irksome daily events in many modern careers is finding a parking place. If that annoys you and pushes you onto the negative side, then you must summon positive energy and devote your time and thought and every other resource you can muster into solving that problem. Get committed to it.

If it sounds absurd to commit yourself to finding the perfect parking place, then quit worrying about it. Most likely, the sun will rise tomorrow whether or not you find a convenient parking spot.

If making a division profitable is your challenge, then stay with it. Focus on that—not on office politics or on what some other division manager is doing.

Once you're in the game, stay in it. You try to pick the challenge: That's the time for analysis, and perhaps withdrawal—it may be something that would require you to master too many new skills too quickly to meet the deadlines. But once you're in there, go after it with everything you can muster. You won't tank and you'll rarely choke.

The essence of responding properly to challenges comes down to this:

1. Learn to control your Internal Energy State regardless of external stress.
2. Understand how to be at your best and how to commit yourself 100 percent to an effort.
3. Evaluate your performance without making excuses. If it didn't work, you gave it your best and you owe no apologies to anyone, especially yourself.

NOTHING UP THE SLEEVE

This isn't a trick.

Getting into the High Positive enables you to perform at the upper range of your skills. But if you don't have those skills in the first place, you certainly can't exercise them. If you don't know a P-E report from a P-and-L statement, being mentally tough will not make you a financial expert; if you've never held a racket, the High Positive won't make you a world-class tennis player.

Further, if you don't have the stamina, then it doesn't matter how enthusiastic you are about meeting a challenge. Being in the High Positive musters your physical and mental resources, but the resources have to be there.

If you're like most performers, though, you know how to do what you do. You want to do it better, and to do it well consistently. And that's where being able to get into the High Positive makes all the difference.

A BIT OF SCIENCE

The four Internal Energy States represent a simplification of the human emotional and nervous system. Every such explanation of humanity is a simplification—from the Freudian id, ego, and superego to the behaviorist's stimulus and response to Jungian archetypes.

Much of our work with performers—from athletes to managers to mechanics to entrepreneurs—and our development of the four Internal Energy States is based upon a branch of science known as psychobiology—a study of emotional states, perception, behavior, and the chemistry of the nervous system.

From a functional standpoint, it is useful to look at the human mind as a combination of three brains, representing the evolution of the central nervous system.

At the most basic level is the "R-complex" (an abbreviation for reptilian complex), called so because a similar structure forms the major part of a reptile's brain. The R-complex is the oldest neural center. Anatomically, it is essentially a swelling at the top of the spinal cord, and it processes ritualistic and reflexive actions. When you jerk your hand away from a hot dish on the stove, or when the pupils in your eyes contract in sudden bright light, those are reflexive actions, processed in this part of the brain. Behavior controlled by the R-complex is very deep and ingrained, and thus difficult to change.[9]

The neocortex, the outer portion, forms about 85 percent of the mass of the human brain; it is the "gray matter." What you normally think of as thinking—reading, writing, verbalization, analysis, recognition, and so forth—takes place in the neocortex, which is more highly developed in humans than in any other creatures, with the possible exception of some dolphins and whales.[10] As you read this, the retinas in your eyes pick up the differences between the light and dark areas on the page. These impulses are conveyed to the occipital lobe at the rear of the brain, where patterns are discerned. The signals travel to the frontal and prefrontal lobes, where you transform the words into meaning.[11] All this takes place in the neocortex. The neocortex has two halves, a left and a right, each of which can process information differently—a recent discovery that has spawned great interest in "left" brains and "right" brains.[12]

Between the R-complex and the neocortex lies the limbic system. It got its name because it sits at the border, and *limbus* means border in Latin. It is sometimes called the paleomammalian brain or the visceral brain. It was once called the "rhinencephalon" (nose brain) because its sole known function was processing odors. But that's only a minor part of the limbic system's function. One of its components, the hypothalamus, contains the mind's pain and pleasure centers. Another, the appestat, determines whether or not you feel hungry. The hippocampus, working with other portions, issues signals of rage and fear.[13]

Impulses to and from the higher brain and the body pass through the limbic system, and the limbic system directly controls the body's autonomic nervous system—those routine matters like breathing, digestion, heartbeat, and blood distribution—as well as the facial muscles. That is why internal emotions are apparent in your pulse and respiration, as well as in your facial expressions.[14]

The glands and centers of the limbic system communicate chemically among themselves and with other portions of the body. The chemicals come in two general categories: neurotransmitters and hormones. Neurotransmitters relay messages between nerve cells; a certain kind of cell will respond only to a certain neurotransmitter. Neurotransmitters work only in the nervous system. Some hormones perform much the same function—conveying messages—but hormones are carried in the bloodstream. Some chemicals, such as norepinephrine, are both hormones and neurotransmitters.[15]

Your emotional state is determined by the balance of dozens of these chemicals—epinephrine, norepinephrine, dopamine, serotonin, and acetylcholine are among the most studied—in your central nervous system. For many years, it was believed that this balance was beyond conscious control—that you were stuck with whatever your emotions chose to deal you. Then it was discovered that the chemical balance could be altered with drugs. For decades, people had known that drugs (everything from morphine and cocaine to barbiturates and amphetamines) had an effect but they did not know precisely why—until the discovery of neurotransmitters. Most mood-altering drugs work by changing the action of neurotransmitters—for instance, by blocking their absorption in the receptor across the synapse, or by stimulating the production of greater quantities of neurotransmitters.[16]

Recent research, detailed later in the book, has demonstrated many other effective ways to control your chemical balance. Something as simple as grimacing has been proven to raise the level of epinephrine (adrenaline) and lower the level of serotonin, thus producing all the physical symptoms of fear (elevated pulse, shallow breathing, slowed digestion, etc.). Eating a breakfast high in carbohydrates will raise the level of tryptophan in your bloodstream, which in turn raises the level of serotonin in the nervous system —and that makes you feel more relaxed.

The strategies of mental toughness are no more and no

less than proven ways to control that chemical balance. Most of them have been around for some time (certain breathing techniques go back several millennia), but only in recent years has science discovered precisely how and why they work. Much more remains to be discovered; it's an exciting field that is full of promise. The strategies here will allow you to take advantage of what is already known and proven and apply it to your body, your mind, and your challenges.

GETTING STARTED

Every strategy in this book is explained to one end: to give you a means of moving from one Internal Energy State to another so that you can perform consistently at the top of your range.

That means staying on the positive side as much as possible, but it doesn't mean staying in the High Positive when you're not performing. The Low Positive is the state of rest and recuperation. It is just as important to know how to move into the Low Positive as it is to know how to move into the High Positive.

But none of those strategies will do you much good if you don't know where you're starting from.

Your first strategy, then, is to become familiar with how you feel and respond in each of your four Internal Energy States. Everyone is different: Some people, in the High Negative, merely snarl; others feel compelled to attack fellow citizens with crowbars.

To begin, copy this page, and write down your most memorable times in each state (the High Positive hour when you were brilliant, the High Negative saloon brawl, the Low Positive week in Hawaii, etc.). Write how each occasion felt. How intense was it? How energized did you feel? How pleasant was it? Were your muscles relaxed or tense?

HIGH POSITIVE *(Finest Hour)*

LOW POSITIVE *(Most Pleasant Relaxation)*

HIGH NEGATIVE *(Fear and Loathing)*

LOW NEGATIVE *(Depressed and Defeated)*

Now that you're familiar with your extremes in these states, begin recording your Internal Energy State several times each day: an hour after you get up, mid-morning, just after lunch, late afternoon, and after dinner. Whenever you notice a major shift in your mood, note that as well.

Being aware of your Internal Energy States is essential, because the strategies of mental toughness are designed so that you can move from state to state. Unless you know what state you're in and what state you want to be in, those strategies won't do much for you.

To keep track, you might use this chart or something similar for a few days:

DAILY ENERGY MONITOR

Date _____

Time _____ Time _____
Activity _____ Activity _____

High Positive	High Negative	High Positive	High Negative
Low Positive	Low Negative	Low Positive	Low Negative

Time _____ Time _____
Activity _____ Activity _____

High Positive	High Negative	High Positive	High Negative
Low Positive	Low Negative	Low Positive	Low Negative

Time _____ Time _____
Activity _____ Activity _____

High Positive	High Negative	High Positive	High Negative
Low Positive	Low Negative	Low Positive	Low Negative

Place an X in the box for the appropriate energy state.

3
ATTITUDE:
Emotion Follows Thought

IDEAL PERFORMANCE STATE: MOOD CONTROL

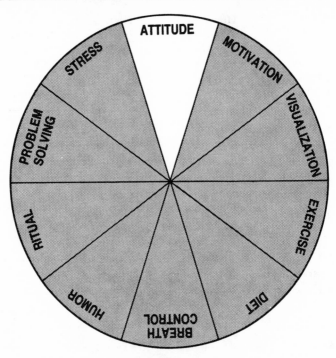

STRATEGIES

Develop a positive attitude.

Top performance is a result of being in a positive emotional state.

Positive emotion follows positive thought.

Positive thinkers make better performers.

A positive attitude is vital to any demanding endeavor. When Verity Lambert, head of production at Thorn EMI Films in Great Britain, puts together a team to produce a new film, her major criterion for whom she will select is not experience—"I like to give people opportunities to move up." It is "enthusiasm. I think enthusiasm encompasses dedication, because people who are very, very enthusiastic about ideas are dedicated to getting it done and making it work."[1]

For as long as sport has been enjoyed, coaches have told their athletes to develop a "good attitude." As the coaches' saying goes, "Attitudes are the stuff of which champions are made." When teams have negative attitudes, they don't play well and they don't win. With the enthusiasm that accompanies a positive attitude, everything else becomes possible.

Lee Iacocca, fired as president of Ford and joining Chrysler, faced imminent bankruptcy—what could have been the largest business failure in American history. He recruited new executives. "Only guys of a certain temperament could hack it. It was more than a challenge—it was an adventure. And in all the travail, nobody ever got weak in the knees. There was no self-doubt. There was no wringing of hands."[2] They had a positive attitude that something could be done.

Neither in sport nor in business have we found a top performer who, in the judgment of those with whom he performs, is a negative thinker or carries a negative attitude. Top performance and negative attitudes simply do not go together.

Consistent high-level performance is the result of discipline, especially disciplined thinking. Disciplined thinking produces a perception of the world that is both realistic and positive. Top performers don't wear rose-tinted glasses; they are fully aware of the challenges they face, and they don't avoid the real world. But with a positive attitude, they know they will find a way to meet those challenges.

Because Internal Energy States are a reflection of your emotional and mental climate, each state has characteristic emotions and thought patterns.

INTERNAL ENERGY STATES AND THE RELATIONSHIP BETWEEN THOUGHTS AND EMOTIONS

High Intensity

HIGH POSITIVE		HIGH NEGATIVE	
Energy without tension		*Tension with energy*	
Thought	Emotion	Thought	Emotion
Can-do	Enthusiasm	Must do	Vengeance
Challenge	Excitement	Too much	Disgust
Inspiring	Delight	Irritating	Anger

Pleasant _____ **Unpleasant**

LOW POSITIVE		LOW NEGATIVE	
Neither energy nor tension		*Tension without energy*	
Thought	Emotion	Thought	Emotion
Ease off	Relaxation	Hopeless	Depression
Placid	Serene	Boring	Ennui
Humor	Pleasure	Over-whelmed	Burn-out

Low Intensity

THE IMPORTANCE OF POSITIVE THINKING

There are good reasons for the sustained popularity of the Norman Vincent Peale ethic, as propounded in his best-selling book *The Power of Positive Thinking*. Not only has it been in print for more than thirty years, but the shelves of bookstores continue to groan under the growing mass of books about positive thinking. There are good reasons for this sustained public interest, and they go down to the roots of biochemistry.

Stop for a moment and think about what's happening in the world at this moment. Within your city, children are being beaten. Across the continent of Africa, thousands of people will die of starvation today. One hundred and thirty-seven Americans who were alive this morning will be dead tomorrow, thanks to auto accidents. Go on for three minutes of this—pick up the morning paper if you have any trouble coming up with depressing thoughts—then look in a mirror and see how the flush of your skin has changed. But your paleness is only one visible part of how you changed in response to negative thoughts. Your pulse isn't the same, and neither is your respiration. Your internal chemical balance has been tilted by negative thoughts.

Now think about the wonderful times in your life, when you laughed hard and loud, when there was joy at real accomplishment. Spend three minutes on the positive side, and see how you feel. Your internal chemistry has changed again, in response to positive thoughts.

The principle is simple but it has vast implications when applied to performance.

MAKING THE BALANCE

The biochemical changes that occur as a result of positive emotions make you different: faster, smarter, better at solving problems, more relaxed, calmer, yet full of energy.

Those changes start with a positive attitude: "Despite what I have been told about emotions, I can change my emotional state." Then comes the essence of mental toughness: "My attitudes and my emotions are intimately connected, and I assume full responsibility for my attitudes." Assuming a positive attitude leads to an improved emotional state, reflected in measurable physiological and neurochemical changes, where you perform at your best.

The process starts with a positive approach, which has several manifestations.

Realistic Confidence: Traced back to its roots, confidence means "with faith."[3] To perform confidently is to perform with faith in your abilities.

Top performance is a mere fantasy if the necessary skills are not present; a "faith" based on what isn't there is what the confidence man sells.

Generally you have already developed the skills that you need for your performances. Performing in the proper emotional climate means that you will summon those skills and exercise them to the best of your ability. Your positive attitude about those skills and your confidence in your own abilities—"I know how to do this"—help bring about the desired emotional climate. This confidence expands into the other attributes of top-level performance.

One characteristic of peak performance is the knowledge that you will never run out of options. Come what may, you've got something you can try. You have a positive attitude—you know you can do it. Knowing you can do it means that you have the confidence to try it another way if your first response hasn't worked, instead of throwing up your hands and succumbing to despair.

A related characteristic is a willingness to experiment. You will try different approaches; you are attentive to how well they work or why they don't work, and by experimenting, you develop a repertoire of options. It takes confidence to experiment, but the process builds more confidence because you learn more about your own abilities.

Honest Commitment: To bring forth your best, you have to believe that a challenge is worth meeting. If you don't care, you can go through the motions of performance, but you'll be light-years away from your best.

An honest belief that a challenge is worth your time and energy brings forth a positive attitude, which in turn provides the emotional energy to help meet that challenge. If

you don't think a job is worth doing, you won't have that
internal energy. Every aspect of the challenge will be a
horrible struggle. Further, your negative attitude will lead
to negative emotions, which can be reflected in negative
physical states—everything from headaches to ulcers to
hypertension to premature death from a myocardial in-
farction.[4]

If you don't believe in what you're doing, either find a
way to believe in it so that you do have a positive attitude,
or find something that you do consider worth your time
and energy.

Consistency: As the saying goes, "Even a blind pig finds
an acorn once in a while." Almost everyone will experience
moments of success and accomplishment, and those moments certainly produce a positive attitude. But the attitude produced this way will last only until the next challenge
comes. Relying on success alone to produce a positive attitude means that you are allowing external forces, which
you cannot always control, to determine your internal emotional climate. The result is inconsistent performance. To
perform well consistently, then, you have to produce your
positive attitudes internally, by means which you control,
rather than allow your emotions, and hence your ability
to be at your best, to be determined by external factors.

NORMAL NEGATIVISM

No one is born with a positive attitude; top performers
develop theirs. For top performance, a positive attitude is
always as important, and generally more important, than
any particular skill. No matter how well you know the skills
of your career, you've got too much sense to apply them
to a challenge if you don't believe it will produce good
results. A positive attitude is the reality-based belief that
you can produce good results.

We won't kid you. It's not easy to develop a positive

attitude in most environments, because most environments emphasize the negative.

In school, for instance, you were measured against an arbitrary standard and judged by how far you fell short of that standard. If you came up only 3 percent short, you got a 97 and an A. If you were 21 percent short, it was an 79 and a C. The feedback system—which told you how well you performed—was based on negatives. The system encouraged you to avoid the penalties of failure, rather than to seek the rewards of excellence.

Unfortunately, most career environments aren't much different. They reflect society at large. The information flow centers on the negative—if you want to confirm that, check this morning's newspaper or the evening news on TV. For every account of outstanding accomplishment, you find hundreds of negative examples: drivers who weren't in any condition to drive, politicians who don't think that the laws they make should apply to them, products made by people who wouldn't themselves use those products.

Negative is normal. Negative thoughts lead to negative emotions, and so anxiety, boredom, anger, depression, and fatigue are normal. Losing is normal; even the best performers lose more often than they win—but they win more often than those normal performers who are suffering from anxiety, boredom, anger, depression, and fatigue. Those negative emotions lead away from performance and directly to sloppy thinking and inappropriate responses.

When you have a positive attitude, you seldom respond the way that everyone else responds. You face tremendous social pressures to do what they're doing, to think as they think, to fit in—to be an also-ran.

The world is a powerful conditioner. It's working on you all the time—negativity is normal, positivity is abnormal. To win, you must train to beat that external conditioning, to overcome the brainwashing exerted by a powerful world of negative influence. You must follow a separate path.

BRAINWASH YOUR OWN DIRTY LAUNDRY

Tom Gullikson is a tennis professional. At one point in his career, he had an awful time with tie-breakers. He'd play well from game to game, but if the set ended in a tie-breaker, Gullikson was in trouble. So much trouble that the tie-breaker was generally a mere formality; he lost almost every one.

Gullikson got so keyed-up and nervous about tie-breakers that he started to hate them. This hatred spread and infected his entire play; as set scores got closer and closer to ties, his play became nervous, edgy, and tight.

More practice wasn't the answer. His skills were great. And it's impossible to simulate a pressure-laden tie-breaker in practice, so there was no way that practice could eliminate his anxiety.

The only answer for him was to somehow change his attitude about tie-breakers.

Gullikson brainwashed himself to do it. He hung signs throughout his home that proclaimed "GULLIKSON LOVES TIE-BREAKERS." Every time he came home he was forced into reading GULLIKSON LOVES TIE-BREAKERS. Through every day, he repeated and repeated GULLIKSON LOVES TIE-BREAKERS.

Maybe it sounds like overkill. If you ran into him in a restaurant, he was likely to be mumbling GULLIKSON LOVES TIE-BREAKERS to himself, or scribbling GULLIKSON LOVES TIE-BREAKERS on a napkin. From a miserable record in tie-breaking situations, Gullikson won nine out of eleven after his self-induced brainwashing. If it wasn't love, it was close enough.[5]

Gullikson's brainwashing was not in any essential respect different from that used on American prisoners of war during the Korean Conflict. As soon as the men were in camp, they started getting the constant messages: "Your country has deserted you. Your wife is with another lover while you're in this stupid war. Your leaders are fools and they don't care about you. You have been betrayed."

At first they laughed it off. But the messages continued and continued and continued. Eventually the prisoners' attitudes changed; some captives refused to return to their homes after the armistice was signed.[6]

A simple message, hammered at you time and time again, will change your attitude. If it didn't, there wouldn't be ads on television.[7] It's the way you are built, and you can't change that.

But as Tom Gullikson demonstrated, you can use brainwashing to work for you and for your own purposes; it doesn't have to be used on you for someone else's purposes.

To do that, you have to identify your problem. What exactly is it that's impairing your performance? That's usually much simpler for an athlete like Gullikson to pinpoint than it is for performers in other arenas.

You have to find the specific factor that upsets your emotional balance and thus degrades your performance. Whatever it is, it must be something you *have* to deal with, something you can't easily get out of—because if you can avoid it, you should. Brainwashing yourself takes a lot of time and energy, and there's no reason to go to all that trouble if there's a simpler way to solve the problem. To put it another way, nobody likes getting called by bill collectors. The preferred strategy is to avoid the calls by paying your bills, not to find a way to enjoy being dunned.

Your problem could be someone whom you have to deal with now and then. You can't get out of dealing with Mr. Pest, but you feel angry and disgusted every time you do, and it throws off everything else. It might be those distractions that you can't avoid—you're not in a position to have your phone calls held off, and every time the phone rings, it annoys the living hell out of you because you're trying to focus on something else. There's a world full of negative possibilities: Isolate the one that irks you.

Then find some short and simple message. It doesn't have to be "I love Mr. Pest" when there aren't two chances on earth that you'd ever love Mr. Pest; "I can handle Mr.

Pest" is sufficient. "I love to stay in touch" might be appropriate for the telephone annoyance, though.

Whatever it is, make it short and simple, and then be thorough about getting the message across to yourself. Use signs, messages, tapes, chants—anything you can think of. Your acquaintances and co-workers will think you're abnormal, and they'll be right; normal people (losers) don't take positive personal action to change their attitudes. It will take time, but the message will eventually soak through to your innermost emotional recesses, changing your attitude and thus your responses and performance.

It changed Gullikson's attitude. Instead of thinking "Oh, no, not another damned tie-breaker that I'm going to blow," he responded by thinking "I love tie-breakers." He wasn't nervous and edgy any more, and his performance improved by several orders of magnitude.

Brainwashing yourself will give you a positive attitude toward those unwelcome contingencies that you must deal with.

The formula for training (positive brainwashing) is simple:

1. Identify your negative attitudes. What habits of thought consistently produce negative thinking?
2. Repeat the attitude you want to acquire, over and over and over. Chant it, sing it, write it, read it. Do it until it's in you.
3. Say "STOP" every time an undesirable negative thought enters your mind. Replace it immediately with a positive thought.

BEYOND BRAINWASHING

There are other ways to change your attitudes, and one of the most powerful is to use body language. By arranging your muscles in certain ways, you can cause powerful changes in your emotional states.

To see how this works, hold your face as if you were deeply frightened. Raise your eyebrows and pull them together. Now raise your upper eyelids. Stretch your lips horizontally, back toward your ears.

Hold this position for a minute or so, and you won't be the same person you were when you started to read this chapter. No longer will you be relaxed, comfortable, and adjusted to your environment. Instead, your breath will be irregular and shallow. Your face will go pale and your skin will cool as blood moves from the surface to the large skeletal muscles, which grow more tense by the moment. Your pupils will dilate and your eyes will become more sensitive to motion. Your heart will beat faster and your blood pressure will rise. In the deeper regions of your central nervous system, the chemical balance changes as epinephrine (adrenaline) enters your bloodstream and begins to transmit impulses among your brain's emotional control centers.

By any measure known to science, you are in a state of fear if you hold this facial expression. Yet you're reading this book, not Stephen King or Edgar Allan Poe. Something as insignificant as the way you arrange your facial muscles changed your emotional state and thus your body chemistry. Consequently every other part of you, from the dilated pupils to the changed breathing to the taut muscles within your feet, was also affected.

It is generally thought that you smile because you feel good. That's true, but so is the reverse. As we will see, recent scientific research has proven that you can feel good because you smile.

EMOTIONAL CONTROL

Performing at your best means that you are in the proper emotional state when you perform. So far, so good, but how do you control your emotional state by conscious thought? From experience, you know it's more complicated than consciously thinking "I'm going to feel good." That sometimes works, but not often enough to be very reliable.

If your emotional state, and hence your ability to be at your best when you need to be, is to be controlled, then there has to be some way to communicate the conscious decision—the attitude you want to have—to the centers in the mind and body that determine emotion.

Emotional states have measurable and specific physical characteristics, which explains the reasoning behind the polygraph—the "lie detector." The polygraph doesn't test for truthfulness; instead, it measures pulse, respiration, blood pressure, and sometimes muscle tension and skin electrical resistance. All those change when someone is under stress—angry or afraid. Telling a lie puts most people under stress; the polygraph records the resulting physical changes.[8]

FACING UP TO IT

Nowhere is your emotional state more closely reflected than in your face, thanks to the way that the brain is wired.

The brain's limbic system is the seat of emotion, and it controls the facial muscles. Without a conscious effort to the contrary, your facial expression, more than any other physical attribute, is a reflection of your emotional state. Such conscious efforts take a lot of effort for most people—which explains why a skilled poker player pays more attention to the faces at the table than the faces on the cards, or why the best actors and actresses can command astronomical sums for their work.

As nearly as researchers can tell now, the human brain automatically expresses emotions by signaling the facial muscles—it's something built in, and it is apparent very early in life. Babies smile when they're happy, and that

occurs months before they have the fine muscle control
necessary for similar learned behavior, like speech.[9]

REVERSING THE FLOW

So you smile when you're happy, grimace when you're
angry, and frown when you're upset. But it turns out that
the transmission of nerve signals runs both ways. That is,
you can feel better as a result of smiling, become angry
merely by grimacing, and get annoyed just by frowning.

This might sound absurd, but it was confirmed in a series
of experiments at the School of Medicine at the University
of California at San Francisco in 1983.[10]

Research subjects were wired to machines similar to
polygraphs, and were videotaped as their pulse, skin temperature, skin electrical resistance, and muscle tension were
measured second by second.

In one phase of the study, the subjects were told to
arrange their facial muscles in certain ways—the fright-
ened-face instructions we gave you earlier are taken from
that experiment. In another phase, the subjects were asked
to relive emotional experiences.

A facial expression associated with happiness—smiling
—produced the same physical changes as did reliving a
pleasant emotional experience. A fearful look, held for ten
seconds, caused the same tenseness in the muscles and
drop in skin temperature as an actual fearful experience.
This also held for professional actors—no matter how
practiced you are at controlling your facial expression, the
expression will be reflected physically in the same way that
an emotional feeling affects the body and its ability to
perform.

Further, adopting a facial expression changes your emotional state very quickly. It took thirty seconds of reliving
a frightening experience to produce the same changes that
occurred with ten seconds of grimacing.

GRIN AND CONTROL IT

This insight into the brain's programming gives you a powerful strategy for getting into the emotional state that will allow you to perform at your best.

Thinking "I want to do this right" is not going to help much if you're tense, bored, or afraid. You can think that all day, but of itself such thinking will not change your emotional state. You'll still be tense, bored, or afraid, and you won't be able to perform at your best. The message isn't getting from the conscious centers of your mind to the emotional centers. Words are a wonderful way to communicate, but this is one place where they don't do the job.

But you can use body language to communicate between parts of your nervous system and thus change your emotional state. You can start by thinking "I want to do this right." Then you assess your current Internal Energy State, and adjust it so that you can perform at your best. Changing the expression on your face is a powerful and rapid way to change your emotional balance—to communicate what you want into what you are.

Put on a confident smile and you will feel secure and confident. Look angry for a few seconds, and you'll feel angry. Frown, and your entire nervous system will frown with you. Your emotional state reflects your face every bit as much as your face reflects your emotional state.

This is something that you've always known how to do —and now you know how to put it to work.

PHYSICAL BEARING

The research at the University of California School of Medicine demonstrates how moving a small part of the body can produce substantial emotional and physiological results.

Changing your facial expression offers a rapid way to change your internal emotional balance, but it's only one aspect of internal communication with body language. Those researchers in California wouldn't have had to travel very far to see a dramatic exhibition of the same effect, on a much vaster scale.

That occurs down the coast at Camp Pendleton, where the U.S. Marine Corps takes young men from all parts of the country, from all walks of life, and in twelve weeks transforms them into disciplined soldiers.[11]

When you think about it, it becomes apparent that what happens at boot camp must be very powerful.

Those young men have had eighteen or twenty years of psychological conditioning. Most of them are fairly talented at slouching, hanging out, looking for girls, eating huge quantities of pizza, and otherwise satisfying themselves. They come from an environment where they were supposed to ask questions, not obey instinctively and instantly. Most of them were reared amid an ethical system that teaches "Thou shalt not kill." And in less than three months, everything changes. They're purposeful, they respond instantly to orders, and they can kill on command.

How does the Marine Corps so quickly and effectively transform its recruits?

They do go to a few classes, where they learn Corps history and tradition, first aid, and how to maintain and fire their weapons. But that intellectual knowledge, valuable as it may be, does not turn MTV watchers into soldiers.

The Marine Corps does it by making them act like soldiers for twelve weeks. The Corps doesn't care what they're thinking—all it cares about is how they act. They stand like soldiers, walk like soldiers, move like soldiers, eat like soldiers. They begin to think like soldiers and then they are soldiers.

We are not saying that mental toughness means becoming a good soldier; it's an honorable calling, but not one suited for everyone, nor is a military approach suitable for most civilian performances. We are saying that the technique which produces such powerful and substantial changes is a valuable technique.

Act as though you are what you want to be, and you will become what you want to be.

How does a confident person act? One stands tall, one speaks with authority, one stays in control. If you stand tall, speak with authority, and stay in control—in short, if you act like a confident person—then you will become a confident person.

Body and mind are so closely linked that control of one leads to control of the other. Thinking "I must be confident" is only the start, because words cannot carry that message where it must go to be effective.

The strategy instead is to think "I must be confident. I cannot make myself confident. But I can control my posture and voice, so I'll control them so that I look like a confident person." The eventual result is confidence. You used body language to carry the message, to connect the centers of willful action in an accessible part of your mind to the centers of emotional control in an otherwise inaccessible part of your mind.

The process doesn't happen overnight; in a disciplined and closed environment like boot camp it still takes weeks, and it can take much longer in an open setting where you don't have a drill sergeant screaming in your face every time you slip up.

On the other hand, you'll be using a proven process to build yourself into what you want to become. The process is so powerful that it transforms the unwilling; its powers are that much greater with the willing.

Your environment gives you plenty of reasons to feel negative, and that's the normal response. When you feel that response, you can use the Marine technique to advance you to your goals. No matter how negative you feel, act positive. Fake it. Fake it with every part of you at your command. It's only an act, but act it as well as you possibly can.

You will become what you have pretended to be.

STAYING IN TOUCH WITH REALITY

So much that has been written about positive attitudes seems to ignore reality. It's all quite inspirational, but you start to get the idea that a positive attitude, in and of itself, will change things.

It won't.

Having a positive attitude does not mean smiling blithely while things fall apart around you. It doesn't mean ignoring negative situations or persuading yourself that all is well when all isn't well. It means being aware of the situation and responding to it.

It is mental sloth to believe that if everyone had the right attitude, the problems of the world would be solved overnight. The most preposterous example is a belief that something as serious as famine can be cured by mere mental gymnastics.[12] The problems of the world are very real problems, and they won't go away just because people adopt a certain mind-set.

Performance solves problems.

Attitude doesn't.

Of itself, an attitude doesn't change anything out there in the arena that you perform in. Developing and maintaining a positive attitude is not an end in itself, but an essential step toward more effective performance.

4

MOTIVATION:
Purpose And Passion

IDEAL PERFORMANCE STATE: MOOD CONTROL

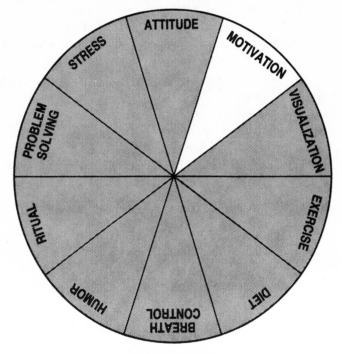

STRATEGIES

Discover the source of your passion.

Love the battle more than the outcome.

J immy the Greek may have put it best: "The thing I love best in the world is playing and winning. Second best is playing and losing."[1] The joy comes from the playing. Winning makes it better, but it's always good with the right motivation.

Everything starts with motivation. It's why you do something. And it has everything to do with performance. The right motivation empowers you to be at your best; inappropriate motivations make your journey nearly impossible.

Assume, for a moment, that you're not feeling well and you need to consult a physician. How would you want that physician to be motivated?

Do you want him treating you because he likes the power and money that a physician can command? Or maybe you'd prefer a negative motivation—the physician works out of a clinic, and he'll lose his position, and fall behind on his home and car payments, if he doesn't treat you. Would you want him interested in your case just because he'd gain professional esteem by writing it up in a medical journal?

Or would you prefer that he treat you because he likes to see his patients regain their health as a result of his talents and skills?

To ask these questions is to answer them. Great performances are not motivated by external factors, but by an internal passion, a joy in the performance itself.

The physician might have shown up in the office that morning because he wanted to make his yacht payments, or because he had once signed a contract that said he would show up, or because he couldn't think of anything else to do that day. None of that necessarily has any bearing on how he performs—if, once he starts to perform, he is internally motivated to perform at his best.

Most material about motivation deals with the external factors that start a performance: money, recognition, fear, etc. But what motivates you to start performing doesn't matter all that much. What motivates you *while* you perform is what determines the quality of your performance.[2]

Mental toughness is the ability to summon the internal motivation necessary for being at one's best, regardless of the initial motivation. You might have started to perform because you needed the money, because you thought there would be recognition in it, because you couldn't think of anything better to do, or even because you were scared of the consequences if you didn't perform. None of that is significant if, during your performance, you are motivated solely by the performance.

MOTIVATION, FOCUS, AND PERFORMANCE

Each Internal Energy State has characteristic motivations that determine the focus, and thus the quality, of the performance.

Generally, then, if you cannot shift your motivation to the High Positive during your performance, then you won't be at your best.

Suppose that you are motivated by the outcome. You're doing it because you want the reward. You're playing to win; you're not playing because you like the game. This motivation controls your focus during the performance. You'll be playing the score, not the ball. You'll think more about the commission than the client, or you'll be savoring the prospect of a promotion rather than insuring that the work before you is done properly. Not only does your immediate performance suffer because your attention is in the wrong place, your long-term drive will suffer as well.

When you are motivated solely by the outcome, you are relying on something for motivation that you cannot control. It's external. You don't determine who gets pay raises or promotions; if that's all that motivates you, then you are bound to be disappointed sometimes. An athlete can play an outstanding game and still lose. As the Bible puts it, "The race is not always to the swift, nor the battle to the strong."[3] No matter how swift and strong you are, you won't always emerge on top. If that's your sole motivation,

MOTIVATION AND INTERNAL ENERGY STATES DURING PERFORMANCE

High Intensity

HIGH POSITIVE *Energy without tension* Internal motivation to respond appropriately to the challenge of the moment. The driving force is excellence, quality, and the personal satisfaction in doing the best you know how. Focus is on the present.	**HIGH NEGATIVE** *Tension with energy* External motivation to prove something by the performance. The driving force is the outcome of the performance: to win, to not look bad, to make a ton of money, etc. Focus is either past or future.
LOW POSITIVE *Neither energy nor tension* Internal motivation is to remain at rest. There is no driving force at the moment. There is no passion, but the lack of passion is temporary; you are simply resting.	**LOW NEGATIVE** *Tension without energy* External motivation to avoid further hassles or problems. There is no driving force because you are burned out; you have lost your passion.

Pleasant _____ **Unpleasant**

Low Intensity

you will eventually lose it. And without motivation, you can't perform at all.

Another motivation is fear—fear of the consequences of a performance. You're not playing to win; you're playing to "not lose." You are worried about what will happen if something goes wrong during your performance. This can take many forms, from choking to covering your ass by making sure that there are plenty of plausible excuses for failure. And you'll probably need them.

In any case, the focus during the performance is on something negative—the consequences of failure. And so your goal is not to perform well, but to avoid failure. Eventually, you figure out that the easiest way to avoid failing is to avoid performing. It's safer to sit on the bench, where nothing can go wrong, than to get into the game, where you might fumble. You've lost your motivation; you don't perform.

That's why you cannot be a top performer if you rely on external motivations to propel your performance. There will always come a time when they disappoint you or depress you.

To be a top performer, you must love the battle more than the outcome.

PRACTICAL IDEALISM

That sounds idealistic. Maybe it means something in amateur sports, but it's not how practical professionals reach the top, is it? Aren't they just in it for the money?

Money is important. And professionals pay attention to it. It takes a ton of money to get Jimmy Connors to show up somewhere, and he and his agents can be as hardheaded as any three bankers about the subject. But once that's taken care of, money leaves the picture. Once Connors is on the court and ready to perform, he's motivated by his desire to perform at his best. His rewards then come from meeting the immediate challenges of the performance, not from any enhancements to his checking account.[4]

Virginia Wade is another tennis professional. The first woman to sit on the Wimbledon Committee, she made lots of money and ranked among the world's top ten for more than a decade. Was it the recognition or the money that satisfied her? "I suppose the satisfaction is really of know-

ing that you have—all the technical, physical and mental
things—and then going out and pitting them against somebody else. Just seeing if you can, if you've got enough
strength, enough determination, to overcome obstacles."[5]

No major-league batter we've ever heard of comes up
to the plate and thinks "Let me see, if I get a hit now,
that'll raise my average to .331, and there's an incentive
clause in my contract that if I get over .330 this year, I'll
get an extra $50,000. There's also a good chance I can get
on the All-Star team if I move my average up. So I'd better
get a hit."

And that motivational myth is just as preposterous when
it comes to performances in the arena of business. The
essential motivation for top performers is not the rewards
of money and power and status, or the fear of want or
failure, but the intrinsic act of performing. They love what
they do and that's what motivates them. It's fun.

Harry Helmsley has amassed $5 billion in real estate,
including the Empire State Building. In his view, "It's the
deal that's fun. It's the shaking of the jigsaw and putting
it together."[6]

In just ten years, Diane von Furstenburg parlayed a
$30,000 loan into a $250 million fashion and merchandis-
ing enterprise, making the cover of *Newsweek* in the process. Her motivation? "It's the warmth that you get in the
fruit of your work or in the fruit of your efforts. It fills
you up with a warmth and you wink at yourself, you smile
at yourself."[7]

Robert Holmes à Court, the Australian lawyer who built
an empire of television stations, newspapers, and oil companies, put it this way: "Now I'm just motivated by doing
what I'm doing as well as I can, and I was equally motivated
practicing law. The difference between the two is hardly
noticeable. I could play chess with you and be motivated
in the same way. It's making each move count. You have
to believe it's worthwhile, but you can believe a game of
chess is worthwhile at that time and place. It doesn't have
to be worthwhile in an idealistic sense, just that it's worth

doing and worth doing well. Now every man in the company can apply that criterion to his job; it may be to do the accounts well. . . . People who are just in it for the money —they usually fail."[8]

Consider something that started not much more than a decade ago. A bunch of fanatic hobbyists got together in a garage to swap stories about their mutual interest. They were completely absorbed—they stayed up for nights on end, and some even lost their jobs. Their passion was motivated by curiosity, and it led to one of the most impressive—and sustained—peak performances the world has ever seen.

These fanatics spent day and night on an arcane hobby —trying to build computers at home in their spare time. That's the idea that drove the members of the Homebrew Computer Club of Santa Clara, California. Their motivation couldn't have been money, because in 1975, there was more money in fly-tying or amateur radio—none of the companies that could have built personal computers had bothered to; even they didn't see any market or profit. It couldn't have been social acceptance, because you don't get that if you're spending all your spare time in a drafty workshop holding a soldering iron and peering at oscilloscope traces. It couldn't have been public esteem—nobody outside knew, or much cared, what they were up to.

But they kept at it, motivated by their love for what they were doing. In the process, they founded an industry and forever changed the way that America thinks and works.[9]

Now, there are many devoted hobbyists; this bunch happened to become multi-millionaires. But the motivation, the love of the intrinsic process, is the same no matter what the outcome. In the words of Stephen Wozniak, a Homebrew member and one of the founders of Apple Computer Corporation: "The rewards that drove us were all intrinsic. . . . It's not like you get a better salary or a better title, or more respect at work, or a new car. . . . The Apple I and II were designed strictly on a hobby, for-fun basis, not to be a product for a company."[10]

DEVELOPING PERFORMANCE MOTIVATION

What motivates top performance is not the reward or the outcome, but the performance itself. To put it another way, you must love what you're doing when you perform. If you don't, it won't hold your interest, and you won't perform at your best.

Generally, the strategy that works best is changing your focus. Instead of worrying about the consequences or anticipating the outcome, becoming distracted or worrying about flaws, focus on the performance itself. There is a time to consider the consequences or the outcome, and that time is before, not during, the performance.

By focusing on the moment, on what you're doing at that time, you bring your full attention to the performance —and it will improve.

This shift in focus is sometimes difficult to achieve because we live in a goal-directed society. Setting goals is vital because that determines the direction. Without goals, you're treading water, expending energy but getting nowhere.

Once the goals are set, though, then the process becomes most important. Focusing on the process then makes those goals more attainable.

For instance, suppose you've decided to climb a mountain next weekend. That's your primary goal—to get to the summit. You handle the other pre-performance considerations—a camera to record you at the summit, some cold-weather gear in case the weather goes bad on you, a map marked with the route, and so forth. Once all that is taken care of, you confidently start up the trail. And your performance begins.

If you remain focused on the outcome, you might reach the summit. But it could cloud up—and if all you care about is reaching the summit, then you're going to be on an exposed ridge during a thunderstorm, running a tremendous risk of getting hit by lightning. The summit might be that important to you, but it probably isn't. So you'll turn back. You relied on something beyond your control

—continued good weather—for your motivation. You'll see the outing as a failure.

Or you might be concentrating on the possible consequences. Here you are, wasting your time on this hike, when you should be at home going over some work you brought from the office. You hurry, so that you can get to your other concerns. You don't watch your footing, trip, and twist your ankle. You find yourself making terrible time because the ankle is trying to grow into a pumpkin. Or perhaps you wonder, "What if I don't make it? What if I get too tired and I just can't keep going any more? As it is I can barely breathe and this trail gets steeper by the second. What will I tell people?" So you find excuses. But the more you worry, the less likely it is that you'll ever see the summit.

If, instead, you focus on the essential parts of climbing—the cadence of putting one foot in front of the other, the satisfaction of gaining elevation, the beauty of the views that open up below you, the rhythm of your breathing—soon it doesn't matter if the weather goes bad. Sure, it would have been better if you could have reached the summit, but there will be other days, and you had a good hike anyway. You won't gaze up at the apex, two thousand feet above you, and think, "Why bother? It is so distant and my footsteps are so small." You'll exult in putting one foot after the other, taking your pleasure in the moment-by-moment process. You know you can always take another step. And with enough steps, the summit always appears.

No matter what you try, from real-estate speculation to free-lance writing, you are most likely to reach the top when you focus on the performance itself and draw your rewards from its intrinsic nature. Any other rewards that come along—the satisfaction of sitting at the summit, the profits of a leveraged investment, or the pride in seeing one's by-line in a national magazine—are mere enhancements. Welcome enhancements, to be sure, but still enhancements.

SKIRTING THE LOW SPOTS

You aren't always performing. Your career might be quite demanding, but it still has its routine moments. And other careers don't make demands on your abilities so much as they make demands on your patience. It's mostly routine stuff that somebody has to do. And you're the somebody.

By changing focus, you can sometimes find challenge and stimulation in the routine. But to be honest, there isn't generally a great deal of challenge and stimulation in making three thousand xerographic copies of something, or answering the telephone, or waiting in an airport, or driving to your next appointment. Life offers plenty of unstimulating routine that can get you down and reduce your motivation—if you let it.

You can prevent that from happening by creating a playframe for the routine. Even if it isn't challenging or stimulating, it can still be enjoyable. That keeps you on the positive side of the chart, so that if a challenge does emerge in the routine and you are energized to meet it, you meet it in the High Positive, rather than in the High Negative.

We could go into any number of specific strategies for creating a playframe, but the process was explained once by a master, and there's no way we can improve on his version.

You probably remember reading Mark Twain's *Tom Sawyer*. As the book opens, Tom has just been caught ditching school on a Friday, so Aunt Polly punishes him by making him work all day Saturday.[11]

"Tom appeared on the sidewalk with a bucket of whitewash and a long-handled brush. He surveyed the fence, and all gladness left him and a deep melancholy settled down upon his spirit. Thirty yards of board fence nine feet high! Life to him seemed hollow and existence but a burden. Sighing, he dipped his brush and passed it along the topmost plank, repeated the operation, did it again, compared the insignificant whitewashed streak with the far-reaching continent of Aunt Polly's unwhitewashed fence, and sat down discouraged."

He sat down discouraged for good reason. He was motivated initially by his fear of Aunt Polly's wrath. That got him to the sidewalk with the whitewash, and even started his performance. He then shifted focus toward his assumed goal—getting the fence whitewashed so that he could go have a good time—and realized that it would take eons to paint the fence. The chore was so onerous that Tom couldn't even pay somebody to do it for him for a few minutes. And he was devastated by his fear of consequences —what if one of his friends should see him in such an embarrassing position, having to do chores on a Saturday?

"At this dark and hopeless moment an inspiration burst upon him! Nothing less than a great, magnificent inspiration."

Tom created a playframe. He started having fun with his whitewash brush. After a few minutes of artistic doodling, he was able to change his focus from getting something awful over with to finding a way to enjoy the task before him. He was so successful at creating the illusion that he was enjoying himself that pretty soon he was enjoying himself. Not only that, but every other boy in the village wanted to join the "fun." The fence got whitewashed, and Tom "had a nice, good, idle time all the while."

Every career offers untold fences to whitewash; creating a playframe makes those routine tasks tolerable. And if anyone sees you having all that fun, you'll probably get some help. Your ongoing challenge, then, is to find the fun, the humor, the game whenever the world presents you with a fence and a brush.

WHEN THAT DOESN'T WORK

Creating a playframe is a powerful way to handle oppressive routine and to deal with situations that challenge your endurance rather than your wits.

But there may come times when it doesn't work. You cannot get fired up about what has to be done, you can't enjoy it while you do it, and you can't even think of a way that you might enjoy doing it. You are totally depressed and unmotivated. Whatever you have before you is something you do not welcome doing.

It happens to athletes who lose their spark—they've accomplished whatever they've set out to do in their sport, and they can't get fired up about it any more. If they play, they just go through the motions. They aren't "hungry" any more. It happens to entrepreneurs when they succeed—they're motivated by the challenges of starting an enterprise; the day-to-day necessities of keeping a business going depress them. It's often called "burnout," and it happens to everyone from time to time.

It is usually a signal that you need a break—you should quit performing and take it easy for a while. That isn't always easy to arrange in an environment where the vacation schedule is made up a year in advance. This mental fatigue is almost always accompanied by physical signs, though—backaches, headaches, aches in general, sore muscles—and it explains a great percentage of any day's sick calls. Unfortunately, this fatigue can go beyond a day or two of staying home and loafing.

One study of corporate stress noted one of the surest ways to predict whether someone will come down with a chronic physical illness (chronic doesn't mean serious here; it means persistent, difficult to cure, and to some degree preventing one from performing): Look at what is scheduled for that person. If he faces a big task that he doesn't want to do, his health will suffer. It isn't just what the Army calls "malingering"—it's actual physical illness, resulting from a lack of motivation.[12]

If you find yourself in that situation, it's time to start looking at yourself and rediscovering the source of your passion.

In 1973, Paul Hawken's Erewhon Trading Company was showing a yearly profit of $250,000—not bad at all for a natural foods company that had begun with a storefront in Boston. By age twenty-seven, Hawken, a high-school dropout, was a millionaire who owned warehouses and railroad cars. He had built an empire, but he had also lost his motivation.

The business was thriving, but his marriage fell apart; to settle up, he had to sell Erewhon. By 1974, he had all of $600 and was living in a trailer house, tending a rich man's garden.

Hawken found a new passion: quality garden tools, ones that fit well in the hand and last and last and last. That love grew into Smith and Hawken, now a $3 million business, and stimulated another passion—sharing his knowledge of business trends with local entrepreneurs. That grew into consulting work for major corporations, as well as the excellent book *The Next Economy*. Hawken rediscovered his passions and pursued them.[13]

However successful you may become, you can be in danger of losing your motivation if you're performing in the wrong environment. Although you are basically motivated by internal rewards, the external system must be to some degree consistent with your needs.

A craftsman, no matter how satisfied he is by good workmanship, will run into these problems if he must always perform in an environment that esteems hourly productivity above his patient ways of fiddling with something until it's perfect. An idea-filled entrepreneur who delights in innovative concepts will be performing in the wrong environment if she's in a place devoted to meticulous craftsmanship. Someone whose motivations are not in the workplace—a devoted hobbyist, for instance, who works only to put bread on the table and keep a roof over his head—can enjoy his daily eight hours as long as they're not challenging; he finds his challenges elsewhere. And he's in trouble if the situation changes and the workplace suddenly demands much more of him than he believes it deserves.

If the life you lead is not consistent with what you love to do and how you perform, you're in trouble.

FINDING YOUR PASSION

Staying out of this deadly trap means getting your life in order and making sure that your internal priorities are consistent with your external priorities. What you do must be consistent with who you are and what you really want.

Stop and think for a few minutes. Answer these questions:

Where do I want to be in five years?
If I were told that I had six months to live, how would I spend those six months? What would I want to get done?
Am I deriving any satisfaction out of what I'm doing now?
Am I living life now, or merely preparing for life?
If they didn't pay me to do what I do, would I still do it?
If I won a million dollars in the lottery tomorrow, how would I live? What would I do each day?
If I were to write my own obituary right now, what would be my most significant accomplishment? Is that enough?
What would I really like to do?

The answers to those questions will tell you what you need to know about yourself—your true motivations, your passions, the things you love to do. In a word, your goals.

REACHING YOUR GOALS

When it comes to goals, there's a time for dreaming and a time for hard analysis. You set the goal when you dream, when you imagine what you could be. That's your ultimate motivation.

Then you start to analyze the goal, and in the process, you generally restate the goal. When we asked people at our workshops to set five- and ten-year goals, most of them listed financial independence.

That goal is so close to being universal in this country that it bears closer examination.

What is it in your dream of financial independence that really appeals to you? When you get right down to it, the mere fact of financial independence doesn't necessarily mean what you think it means at first.

Someone with investments to manage may be financially independent, but still be tied down to a tight schedule—and maybe your idea of financial independence meant winters in Florida, summers in the Rockies, and travel to other interesting places during the rest of the year. Your real goal is not financial independence, but the opportunity to travel widely. By changing careers, you might be able to do that starting next week, and avoid all the bother and uncertainty of trying to amass a fortune first.

Another person might look at financial independence as freedom from having a supervisor, as an opportunity to set her own schedule each day. And that's something she could attain by free-lancing in her profession. To you, financial independence might mean the time to devote to your true interests, the things that captivate you—being outdoors, or fiddling with your computer, or working in your shop, or coming up with a perfect spaghetti sauce. Again, a change in career means you can reach your true goal, which isn't financial independence.

So look at your goal in terms of what it really offers you. What do you really want? What do you enjoy doing?

That's your passion. Now you have to find a way to fulfill it, and that's where the incidental techniques of motivation and goal-setting come in.

You must break down your long-term goal into short-term goals, each of which is measurable, attainable, and within your control.[14]

For instance, say your long-term goal is to hold a position of greater responsibility. In a pinch once, you ended up in charge of a major project. It was almost frightening because you were responsible for a lot of things you weren't familiar with. But you loved it—it was exciting the whole time, and you felt flat when you returned to your regular duties. You like the challenges; they motivate you, and you want to face them more often. So you take steps toward that goal by establishing short-term goals.

By measurable, we mean that there is a way to tell whether you've met the short-term goal. You're good at the work you do, but you know that you'll have to be more familiar with finance; more responsibility means being able to see a broader picture. So one short-term goal is to learn the language of accounting. You enroll in a night class; if the teacher is even remotely competent, you'll be able to tell, thanks to your scores in class, how well you are meeting this short-term goal. Further, you know how to focus on the moment—when you're in class, you grasp everything you can there; you don't feel sorry for yourself because you're not doing something else. You're doing what you want to be doing.

By attainable, we mean that a goal is something you can realistically achieve. Your next step toward your goal might be to give yourself a better appearance, because that's important in your organization. Losing weight is an attainable goal—getting taller isn't. So make sure that your incremental goals represent things that are within reach. It's good if you must strain to reach them, but make sure you can reach them. The summit is an impossible distance away, but you can always take one more step toward it. Who's to say whether the summit is attainable? But you know that the step is.

Most important, the incremental goals must be within your control. You might want someone to notice your good work—but you can't really control that. You can control another factor, though: You can make sure that you are doing good work.

Setting your long-term goal, and then proceeding step by step through measurable, attainable, and controllable incremental goals, provides another powerful source of motivation: success. It's positive feedback.

We first noticed the importance of positive feedback

when working with tennis professionals, and it was by accident. We were videotaping their practice sessions so they could review their form later. But we picked up the sound as well.

Most of what we heard when players missed shots was along the lines of "You dummy!" "You moron!" "You blind halfwit!" "A four-year-old can do better than this." "What the hell am I doing out here?"

That's what they were telling themselves about themselves. We found that their performances improved dramatically when they stopped the self-abusive feedback, and started thinking about the positive—what they were accomplishing, instead of what they weren't. They still missed shots—everybody does—but instead of dwelling on them and thereby depressing themselves, they were able to be excited by the opportunity offered by the next ball.

There are many people in this world who will give you all the negative feedback you will ever need, and likely a great deal more than you need. Unfortunately, there aren't many who'll provide the positive feedback based on real accomplishments. But that's something within your control —at the least, you can stop criticizing yourself as you meet your incremental goals.

Each incremental goal you meet and surmount builds your confidence while it enhances your skills. You feel better about yourself because you know that you are headed in the right direction and that you are making progress in that direction.

MAINTAINING DIRECTION

The direction, that ultimate goal you strive for, is all-important, for it gives meaning and impetus to every aspect of your life. While millions of Europeans died in Nazi concentration camps, Viennese psychiatrist Viktor Frankl lived through Theresienstadt and Auschwitz. The manuscript of a book he had been working on for years was destroyed. His wife and his mother died in the camps. He lost everything that normally keeps people going.

Frankl vowed to live to tell the world of the horrors; his very survival became a moment-by-moment life-and-death performance, and he triumphed to tell the story in *The Will to Meaning*. The essence of human life, he concluded, is the search for a personal meaning, a motivation that fuels every other aspect of existence.

Or, as the philosopher Friedrich Nietzsche said, "If we have our own *why* of life, we shall get along with almost any *how*."[15]

5
VISUALIZATION:
What You See is What You Get

IDEAL PERFORMANCE STATE: MOOD CONTROL

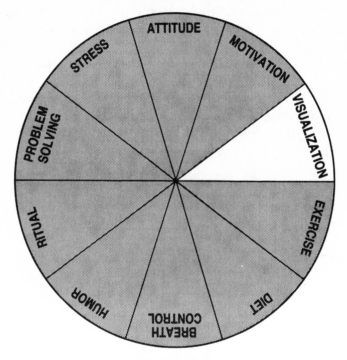

STRATEGIES

Use visualization to provide energy and relaxation through control of emotional states.

Visualization improves performance through mental rehearsal.

Visualization also improves memory and enhances creativity—the ability to identify and solve problems.

The easiest way to realize the power of visualization is to quit thinking about mental toughness or performance under pressure for a few minutes. Think about something more pleasant and stimulating. Sex.

Pick a partner—perfect in form, dark-haired or blonde, fair or swarthy—your choice of the fairest on earth. The sheets are satin, and the surface below you is pliant and supple, embracing you with warmth. Your partner is fervent, fevered, wants you, needs you, would do anything to please you. Your body is flushed and expectant, as sultry, heated, and moist as a tropical night. You feel fingertips entwining your hair, hot breath fanning your cheek, flesh moving against your flesh, sinuous motion, need, urgency, muscles tensing, compelling, demanding . . .

The evocative mental images you form while thinking about sex lead to emotional reactions which are reflected in physical changes—among other effects, your nostrils flare, your pulse quickens, and you feel warmer all over because the capillaries in your skin have dilated to carry more blood.[1]

Such is the power of an internal vision. The chemistry of billions of cells throughout your body—especially those in the central nervous system—changed in response to a phantasm, something you imagined. You produced those images, and their corresponding emotional and physical changes, at an arbitrary time and place; the results had nothing to do with whether your current environment is stimulating or stultifying.

Each Internal Energy State has corresponding mental imagery; you can move from state to state by evoking the proper imagery through visualization. This gives you another tool for controlling your emotional state, and thus your performance.

MENTAL IMAGERY
ASSOCIATED WITH
INTERNAL ENERGY STATES

High Intensity

HIGH POSITIVE	HIGH NEGATIVE
Energy without tension	*Tension with energy*
Images of yourself at your best; superb focused performance, unstrained yet masterful. In control.	Images of yourself violated, harmed, seeking revenge, getting even, attacking, angry, irate.

Pleasant ————————————————— **Unpleasant**

LOW POSITIVE	LOW NEGATIVE
Neither energy nor tension	*Tension without energy*
Images of yourself relaxed, unhurried, calm, pleasant, easy-going.	Images of yourself depressed, bored, afraid, tired, hopeless, powerless, victimized.

Low Intensity

DEVELOPING AN IMAGE BANK

Changing emotions through mental imagery is nothing new. Writers do it all the time; the power of the great novelist is his ability to create scenes so vivid that the reader feels emotionally involved, at turns elated, depressed, inspired, aroused, afraid, worried, fretful, triumphant. Motion pictures and televised drama, because they can display images as well as evoke them, are sometimes even more involving. But if you really want to get involved, create your own "mental movies" for controlling your Internal Energy States.

You have to make your own imagery because you know yourself and how you respond to certain scenes. It isn't effective to generalize or to rely on other people's ideas of what is relaxing or energizing.

At our workshops, we generally demonstrate the power of relaxing imagery by asking people to close their eyes and imagine themselves floating on a tropical lagoon. The scene was utterly relaxing to us and to many others in a metropolitan hotel conference room. But the image was threatening to some people—they didn't know how to swim, and the idea of being out in the water made them feel panicky. A sales representative and weekend mountain climber we know gets into the relaxation state with an image of herself resting triumphantly on an alpine summit; somehow neither of us could be very relaxed while imagining ourselves at the apex of a cold, windy, barren rock spire, no matter how stunning the view.

At the minimum, you need to develop three strong images: relaxed, energized, and your finest hour. Each image must be strengthened and intensified by involving all your senses, so that when you summon it, the effect is overwhelming.

Relaxation Image

For relaxation, recall a time when you were totally at ease, secure, and unworried. Imagine yourself in that setting again. Get a good picture of it—were you in sunlight or shade? Was it day or night? Indoors or out? Bright light or dim? What could you see from where you stood, sat, or lay? Did it hold your interest? What were you wearing? Whom were you with?

Involve the other senses. What did it smell like there? Were there food odors, flower scents, crisp air? Was it warm or cool? How did your body feel—your feet, your hands, the big muscles in your legs? What could you hear? Was it distant or near? Melodic or jumbled? Human speech or mechanical rumblings? What could you touch? Was it hard or soft, hot or cold? Was there a taste in your mouth?

Recall every possible sensation of that relaxed moment; the more you recall, the more powerful the image will be, and the more quickly and easily you can relax when you summon that image. When you do so, the chemistry of your nervous system will change; you will breathe more deeply and the accumulated muscle tension will dissipate.

Energizing Image

For energy, think of something that pumps you up, makes you want to go and keep going. Often, we have found, it isn't sight so much as sound that energizes. For instance, you might feel listless and tired at a nightclub, and be wondering why you didn't leave an hour ago. But then the band plays one of your favorite songs. After three chords, you're ready to dance until dawn.

A communications executive—and a railroad buff—told us that his favorite energizing image was a steam locomotive starting up under a heavy load.[2] Whenever he had trouble staying focused on his work, he'd pause for a few moments and deliberately let his mind wander to a railroad scene from his youth: thick black smoke and steam exhaust barking up the stack as the pistons slowly slid and started to spin the drivers, the intricate pace quickening and the chugs blending together, the train clattering off to its destination. As soon as that scene played in his internal cinema, he could return to his work with a full head of steam.

Similar energizing imagery comes from those at our workshops who are pilots—to fire themselves up, they just recall pulling back on the throttle and feeling themselves climb.

Whether your energizing imagery comes from Bruce Springsteen, steam locomotives, jet fighters, or (most likely) some entirely different source, develop it. Use all your senses to create or recreate the scene so that it is as vivid as you can make it. You'll feel it in physical energy as your nervous system responds to the stimulus.

Finest Hour Image

Your finest hour—when were you most memorably in the Ideal Performance State? When did the elegant response come effortlessly, no matter how intricate or demanding the challenge?

Often, we have found, the most vivid memories of peak performances are those from sports. Perhaps a tennis match where everyone, including yourself later, said you were playing way over your head. Or a softball game in which you went four-for-four and made an over-the-shoulder catch in the outfield that robbed someone of a triple.

It may well have been at work, on the day when a proposal that you'd been defending for two weeks suddenly fell into place. Or the time two difficult prospects finally saw the light; on that day, you could have sold sand to the Saudis. Or the time that you had to overhaul an engine, and all of the parts were at hand and actually fit together on the first try.

Wherever your finest hour occurred, recall it in every detail, with every sense: sight, sound, smell, taste, touch. Etch it into your consciousness so that you can summon it in an instant. When you evoke your images of relaxation, energy, and your finest hour, you change your emotional state—which controls your performance.

Imagery controls your response to reality.

REMOVING NEGATIVES

The ability to visualize the positive does not always remove the negative. But the skill of visualization gives you a conceptual tool for controlling negative emotions. You can visualize them, thus giving them form. Then you can deal with that form in your imagination—you can get rid of it, or replace it with a positive.

To get this control over negative influences, first identify them. What is it that's bothering you today? Is it a reprimand you got yesterday for something that really wasn't your fault? A co-worker who isn't pulling the weight? Being behind on something that should have been done yesterday? Not enough time to do the job right?

Whatever it is, give it an image. An accountant[3] told us she thinks of negative influences as bulldogs, all running about her, snapping and yapping and baring their teeth, requiring so much attention that she can't get where she's going. Then she imagines that the bulldogs all smell fresh meat three blocks away; in moments she is free to get where she's going, unimpeded by those snarling canines. Further, she usually starts laughing because the image is so ludicrous as she visualizes the work-shirking drone at the next desk as a homely bulldog. She has eliminated the performance-destroying negatives and moved to the positive side.

Many top athletes use positive imagery to correct their form after a mistake, finding that the technique improves their mechanics as well as their emotional control. The key to the technique is to replay the incident mentally, but to visualize—not analyze—the correction.

There is a difference. With analysis, you focus on what went wrong: Was I out of position? Did I misread the ball? Shouldn't I have been expecting that? With positive imagery, you instead visualize how it would have been if you had responded perfectly. The goal is to create such a powerful image that you actually trigger the same feelings and emotions that would have occurred if the movement had been executed perfectly.

Visualization thus provides a quick and effective way to eliminate negative emotional influences. Identify the influences, give them an image, and then find a way to dispose of the image.

Some negative emotions are normal and healthy—for instance, grief at the loss of a loved one. One powerful way to cope is to replace the negative imagery—the feeling of loss; the emptiness; the last sight of someone who may have been horribly injured or succumbing to the ravages of disease—with positive imagery. Remember the good times, but remember them intensely. Take time to form the images with every sense.

The feelings of loss are inevitable in a healthy person. But you can maintain your stability by evoking the positive images; this is certainly a nobler way to honor someone's memory. After all, how would you want to be remembered?

IMAGINATIVE REALITY

Mental images seldom bear much relationship to what's going on in the observable universe at the moment, yet thanks to the architecture of the human brain, these immaterial phantasms often affect the emotions with the power of reality.

Most of the information you receive and process is visual; it comes in from your eyes. The brain has a major center set aside for processing images. Images, whether perceived with the senses or summoned from memory, go to the visual cortex. From then on, the brain handles them in much the same way, regardless of their source.[4]

In a test of mental manipulation, for instance, the subjects are presented with something resembling a Rubik's cube, and they memorize the colors of its facets. Once they're familiar with the cube, it is removed, and they have to rely on visual memory. When asked to "turn the cube over" and report what colors they see, it takes them the same amount of time to do this with their stored mental cube images as it would if they were handling a real cube.[5]

All such information, whether from the senses or from memory, is processed by the limbic system. Sensory information from the body goes through the limbic system to reach the brain; commands from the brain to the muscles pass through the limbic system. The limbic system is also the controller of emotions. Emotional state affects the limbic system, which in turn directs sensation and action.

The limbic system responds to mental images in much

the same way that it responds to information from the external world. Dr. Maxwell Maltz has observed that the human brain, at its deeper levels, cannot distinguish between something that actually happened and something that was only vividly imagined.[6]

American psychologist Edmund Jacobson asked people to imagine themselves running; he found small but measurable contractions in the muscles that are used for running.[7] Taking this a step further, Richard Suinn, a sports psychologist at Colorado State University, hooked an alpine ski racer to an electromyograph—a machine that measures muscle tension—and asked the skier to relive, moment by moment, a slalom:[8]

> Almost instantly, the recording needles stirred into action. Two muscle bursts appeared as the skier hit jumps. Additional muscle bursts duplicated the effort of crossing a rough section of the course, and the needles settled during the easy sections. By the time he finished this psychological rehearsal of the downhill race, his EMG recordings almost mirrored the course itself. There was even a final burst of muscle activity after he had passed the finish line, a mystery to me until I remembered how hard it is to come to a skidding stop after racing downhill at more than forty miles an hour.

Emotional responses to imagery are more than minuscule muscular contractions.

When you went to *Raiders of the Lost Ark* the first time, the objective reality of what you saw was simply a series of artfully contrived still images; nothing real threatened you as you leaned back in a comfortable theater seat and waited for the previews to end. The perceptive reality was somewhat different; before the first reel was over, you ducked as an eight-ton boulder roared toward you. Your limbic center reacted to this perceived threat by ordering the glands to pump out some epinephrine (adrenaline); your heartbeat quickened; you felt goose bumps as blood was withdrawn from your skin and went into the big muscles (presumably for pushing that boulder off your chest); you felt your stomach flutter as it lost blood to the big muscles.

All from an image that had no basis in objective reality.

As Nancy Samuels and Mike Samuels put it in their excellent book, *Seeing with the Mind's Eye*, "When a person holds a strong fearful image in the mind's eye, the body responds, via the autonomic nervous system, with a feeling of 'butterflies in the stomach,' a quickened pulse, elevated blood pressure, sweating, goose-bumps, and dryness of the mouth. Likewise when a person holds a strong relaxing image in the mind, the body responds with lowered heart rate, decreased blood pressure and, obviously, all the muscles tend to relax."[9]

The most astounding examples of such control are the swamis and yogis, who can willfully and at request raise and lower their blood pressure, their oxygen requirements, their pulse, or even their body temperature.[10] To become that skilled at such emotional control takes years of disciplined practice, and an American performer need not attain this level of near-perfection. But it is significant that the yogis accomplish and maintain this control through visualization. By evoking internal mental imagery, they control every aspect of their physical response to the world.

To relate relaxation imagery directly to performance, consider what Terry Kennedy, catcher for the San Diego Padres, had to say to sports reporters: "A lot of you guys just don't ask the right questions. I mean, you always come up to a guy after a game and ask what kind of pitch he hit for a home run, or something like that. What I'd like to be asked is what I did to prepare myself for a certain situation or time at bat. I asked Ernie Banks that question once and he said he would think of Lola Falana before going to bat. He did that to get himself relaxed, because he knew what he was likely to see and what he wanted to do when he got up there."[11]

OBSCURING REALITY

The emotional power of images is so strong that they often overwhelm rational thought. Look at a cigarette advertisement. No one, not even the tobacco companies, will argue rationally or scientifically that cigarettes are good for your health. But that impression certainly comes across through images.

The smokers in the full-color magazine ads are not any smokers we know. They don't wake up with a racking cough, or spend their days worrying and wheezing amid the fumes from smoldering ashtrays. They aren't social pariahs scrounging for a spot to practice their addiction. The smokers in the ads present a positive image—calm, collected, in control. Images overwhelm objective reality to the extent that 700 billion cigarettes are sold every year in this county; the tobacco companies spend $400 million a year to create and reinforce those misleading images.[12]

Imagery is often more powerful than logic. Instead of letting other people use it to affect your life, you can develop it to control your own life.

USEFUL BY-PRODUCTS

The process of visualizing requires you to use the right hemisphere of your brain; the left half handles sequential and logical relationships, such as words and numbers, and the right deals with concepts, patterns, and spatial relationships.[13]

Consequently, when you turn words or numbers into images, or when you convert images and patterns into words and numbers, you're using your entire brain—you're going after the challenge with everything you can muster. That's one reason that solutions so often arrive as a result of visualization.

Often, the visualization takes place at a subconscious

level, appearing in a dream that solves the problems which eluded conscious solution.

Friedrich von Kekule, a German chemist of the nineteenth century, struggled with formula and beaker to unravel the structure of trimethyl benzene, an abiding mystery of organic chemistry. It just didn't function the way that most carbon compounds did, and the more Kekule struggled, the more difficulties he found. One afternoon he relaxed before a fire. "My mental eye," he later recalled, saw "long rows, sometimes more closely fitted together; all twinkling and twisting in snakelike motion." Then one of the snakes grabbed its own tail, solving the mystery. Benzene had a ringlike structure; it wasn't linear like the other carbon compounds. "Let us learn how to dream, gentlemen," he later advised his colleagues, "and then perhaps we shall discover the truth."[14]

Something as prosaic as the sewing machine evolved from a similar immaterial origin. Elias Howe had struggled for months to mechanize stitchery, but he couldn't figure out how to get the needle and thread to enter the cloth at the same time. One evening he suffered a nightmare from his obsession. A hostile tribe had captured him, and told him he had two choices: Die at the end of a spear, or produce within twenty-four hours a machine that could sew. Howe broke into a cold sweat and failed. The spears flew toward him. But each spear had an eye-shaped hole in its business end. In the nick of time, Howe awoke, quaking in fright at that awful image of the oncoming spear—with a hole in its tip. And then he realized that he had seen the solution. The hole for the thread had to be at the tip of the needle.[15]

Conscious visualization also leads to discovery. Albert Einstein began to develop the theory of relativity after he visualized what he would see and feel if he could ride on the tip of a ray of light; the equations of atomic energy were the result of this imaginary voyage aboard a light beam.[16] For a century, engineers tried to relate the flight of birds to a flying machine and failed; the Wright brothers visualized a big kite, and founded an industry.[17]

LEARNING TO VISUALIZE

Visualization is like many other skills of emotional control: Once you've developed it, you can deploy it at almost any time and place. But it takes practice to develop it to that level. It's best to start in a quiet place, free of distraction, so that outside stimuli don't overwhelm your internal imagery.

The steps for developing a strong mental image (start with your relaxation, energizer, and finest hour visualizations) are simple:

1. Recall the scene.
2. Close your eyes and develop it.
3. Bring in one sense at a time. Start with what you saw, then move to the sounds, and then the tastes, odors, and other sensations, building the experience to overwhelming proportions.

It is, however, impossible to do this while reading how to do it. If your eyes are focused on the page and you're converting words into ideas, you can't at the same time be visualizing a different scene. We have found two methods to get around this problem.

One is to memorize the steps before you start to practice them.

The other is to rely on another source for direction as you visualize. Get someone to work with you, drawing forth the sensations from your memory so that you can implant them. Or use a cassette recorder. Tell it what you want to do, and then play the tape as you relax with your eyes closed.

As you learn to visualize, you will find other powerful ways to improve your performance with this tool. As you become more skilled, you will be able to visualize in noisy, disruptive, and distracting environments. You will be able to summon the important images—energy, relaxation, and finest hour—whenever you need to change your Internal Energy State.

MENTAL REHEARSAL

Jack Nicklaus didn't go to the golf course for every practice session. He explained, "First I 'see' the ball where I want it to finish, nice and white and sitting up high on the bright green grass. Then the scene changes and I 'see' the ball going there: its path, trajectory, and shape, even its behavior on landing. . . . the next scene shows me making the kind of swing that will turn the previous images into reality."[18]

He isn't the only athlete who realizes that mental practice is as vital as physical practice.

Jean Claude Killy, injured and unable to ski before a race, obtained films of the grand slalom course; his sole preparation was mentally skiing the course before the race. He was the only competitor who had not physically skied the course; he was the only competitor who finished first.[19] Robert Foster, who could not practice for a year, returned to competitive shooting to break his own world record on his first outing. For ten minutes every day of that year, he had mentally practiced his shooting by imagining himself on the range in every situation. The list goes on: Bruce Jenner credits a mental rehearsal of each event for his 1976 gold medal in the decathlon. Bill Russell watched his opponents so closely that he could play "movies" of them in his mind; nothing they did on the basketball court was likely to surprise him. Fran Tarkenton ran through every upcoming game in his mind: "I'm trying to visualize every game situation, every defense they're going to throw at me. I tell myself, 'What will I do on their five-yard line and it's third and goal to go, and our short passing game hasn't been going too well, and their line looks like a wall, and we're six points behind?' "[20]

These mental rehearsals prepare top performers for their performances; by visualizing the likely events in advance, they are confident that they're ready for anything that might come up. They don't get surprised and they don't panic, because their mental rehearsal has prepared them; they always have a repertoire of options developed through mental rehearsal.

Pilot and psychologist Claire Kopp discovered that visualization was a valuable learning tool. "I couldn't seem to get the hang of landing. One evening, disgusted and deep in thought about my landings, I spontaneously began to image a landing. It was fascinating. I then reconstructed each of the day's landings, and visualized the final leg, point of flare, the wind conditions, and where I was looking just before touchdown. Seeing those vignettes, I suddenly began to review my good moves and my errors. The errors stood out in bold relief! . . . The combination of instruction and imagery led to more effective anticipation and better landings."[21]

But you're not a pilot or a professional athlete. Your upcoming performance is a presentation you have to make next week. How do you rehearse for it mentally?

If you're like most Americans, you'd do anything rather than stand before people and give a speech; according to surveys, speaking to audiences is the leading fear (ranking well above bankruptcy and rattlesnakes) of professionals.[22] So you've got a good excuse for spending the week before your presentation in cold-sweat stomach-knotted dread and anxiety.

But you could forego the tension and mentally rehearse instead. Imagine the demanding audience before you: What will they look like? How will they be seated? Where will they be looking? What will they want to know? In your mind, go through your presentation and observe how they respond. Then switch sides and be part of your audience, observing yourself going through the speech. You hear a clumsy transition that could lose the audience; you can fix it. Your conclusion drags because you made your point earlier; you rearrange your presentation.

With mental rehearsal, you improve your presentation. You know what it will look like to your audience, and you know it's good. You're confident and ready when you give the presentation, thanks to visualization.

SWITCHING SIDES

Visualization can improve your powers of persuasion by allowing you to "switch sides"—to imagine that you are the people you must persuade.

A top-selling real-estate saleswoman told us how she uses visualization this way. "Before I meet with people, I try to find out everything I can about them. Then, well this sounds kind of silly, but I pretend I'm them, and I watch myself try to sell the property. As I envision myself as my clients, I ask questions, make objections—anything they're likely to do. So when we meet, I'm prepared. I suppose you could look at this as some sort of sales trickery, but I really can't see it that way. By putting myself in my customers' place, I'm really serving them better."[23]

A free-lance writer uses much the same visualization technique. "Whenever I want to sell to a magazine, I look through several issues. This sounds like some Walter Mitty fantasy, but then I imagine that I'm the editor-in-chief, sitting in an office in Boston or New York, in a meeting with the other editors, planning our articles for the next issue. I imagine the whole scene, and after I play that through, I know just what articles they're going to want to buy. Before I did this, I might have connected on 10 percent of my query letters. Now it's close to 75 percent."[24]

CATASTROPHIZATION

This word hasn't shown up in any dictionaries yet, but it's a useful concept. It means to visualize the worst possible consequence of an effort. Take those nagging and vague fears, and give them form through visualization—make images of what might happen, and how you would cope.

A professional golfer we work with explained that this tactic is his secret weapon.[25] "I walk the course and look at all the godawful places a ball might land—bottomless sand traps, underbrush you have to hack through with a machete, whatever. I imagine that I've really screwed up and put a ball in one of those places. You know what's funny? No matter where the ball is, I can always find a way to play it. So when I get on the course, I'm relaxed. I know I can handle the worst that might happen there."

He converted a vague fear—"What if I don't drive well tomorrow?"—into imagery: a ball in a specific spot. He knew he could handle that.

This process has succeeded for dozens of business people. Many aren't fulfilled in their current positions, but they're afraid to move on to new challenges. The worries may be vague, but they're certainly real. So we ask them to visualize the worst-case scenario that might occur as a result of a decision: What is it that you don't want, but are afraid you might end up with? Will you run out of money for a while? Will you run into another wall somewhere? Will there be a corporate culture that you don't mesh with?

They run through the dismal scenarios; if the worst is something they can handle, then they can make the change with a positive and confident attitude. If it's something they can't see a way to cope with, then they feel better about staying where they are.

In either case, visualization has given them the power to control those nagging anxieties that often accompany challenges. It's a tool that improves decision-making and builds confidence.

JOGGING THE MEMORY

You're hard at work on a project; the information is scattered all over your desk as you grab numbers from here and projections from there. The telephone rings. Then someone comes in. And then you have to keep an appointment. When you return to the project, you can't find some vital paper. You visualize yourself before you were distracted, watch yourself slide that important paper into a basket so it wouldn't get lost—and there it is.

Visualization, because it involves so much of your mental energy—the largest single processing center in your brain is devoted to images—is the most effective tool for enhancing memory. Putting it to work can mean an end to many of those performance-impeding annoyances.

THE LONG HAUL

The ultimate power of visualization lies in your self-image.

How do you see yourself now? As someone overworked and underpaid? Overwhelmed and unappreciated?

What do you want to be?

Form that image of confidence, commitment, and control, again using every sense. See yourself as a top performer in your chosen area, unflappable but totally energized, capable of awesome deeds.

People tend to live up to their own images of themselves. In one famous experiment, elementary-school students, told that they were disruptive and slow to learn, began to see themselves precisely that way; it became a self-fulfilling prophecy. When told that they were capable of superb work, their self-images changed, and they started producing superb work.

Improving self-image is the key to successful coaching in every sport; the players will be as good as they believe they are. One problem with the arenas of the real world is that you seldom get a coach who wants to draw out your best; you get managers, executives, and administrators, who generally have other concerns.

But performance would improve if managers began to think more like coaches. A coach can't go out on the field and win the game; only the players can. All the coach can do is make sure that they're prepared, physically and, most important, mentally. The coach is only as good as his players' performance, so he makes sure his players are confident and have positive self-images. Managers, executives, and administrators are likewise judged most by the performance of their subordinates; it would be in everyone's interest if they paid as much attention to the self-image of their charges as coaches do.

Your self-image is the most important tool in your mental arsenal; it controls your emotions when a challenge appears. If you see yourself as someone who can surmount the challenge, you will.

Becoming a top performer takes more than visualization, but visualization helps you define your goal and gives you an effective tactic for reaching that goal.

What you see is more than what you get. What you see, when you close your eyes and look at yourself, is what you can become.

6
EXERCISE:
Physically Fitter Means Mentally Tougher

IDEAL PERFORMANCE STATE: MOOD CONTROL

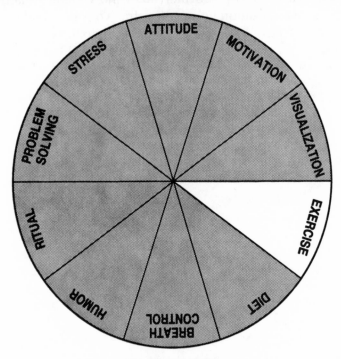

STRATEGIES

Exercise regularly to relax tension, elevate mood, increase confidence, and build mental stamina.

Physical fitness translates automatically into mental toughness.

T raining for the world championship is never easy. This performer's regimen was no exception.

He began with an hour of tennis lessons from a demanding old pro who loved to run him rubber-legged. Then to the gym to lift weights, jump rope, pedal the Exercycle, and punch a 300-pound bag. To build his wind, he jumped into the pool and swam lap after lap underwater.

After he rested from that daily workout, he practiced for his upcoming world championship match.

Although all this took place at Grossinger's in upstate New York, where so many boxers have built themselves for title bouts, this regimen concerned mental combat.

The man was Bobby Fischer. The contest was the world chess championship in 1972, and his opponent was Boris Spassky.

This regimen of physical exercise was not one of Fischer's celebrated quirks. Chess appears to be as cerebral and sedentary as a human pursuit can get. But when grand masters battle, it's physical. In an ordinary six-hour game, a professional will lose four or five pounds. In a twelve-game series, no matter how much he eats between games, he will burn off at least fifteen pounds. The world championship can stretch to twenty-four games spread across ten weeks.[1]

No matter how well the master knows poisoned pawns and queen's gambits and fianchettoed bishops, he cannot deploy his mental skills unless he has physical stamina.

Mental work is physical work. Performance requires energy.

A MISSED CONNECTION

The direct relationship between physical stamina and mental performance seems to have escaped many people who should know better.

Even those who are committed to an exercise program see its benefits as primarily physical—they believe that it pays off only because they reduce their risk of heart attack and they call in sick less often. They feel better with their enhanced strength and confidence. But they seldom see that physical exercise has anything to do with daily performance in a desk-bound career.

Millions of others continue to cherish an assumption as old as it is false. They believe that the mind and body are discrete and unrelated entities; that it's brain versus brawn, mind versus matter, jock versus nerd, always one or the other.

To comprehend the extent to which physical condition influences mental performance requires an understanding of human anatomy. The brain is part of the body, forming about 2 percent of the body's mass. But with only 2 percent of the mass, the brain uses 25 percent of the body's energy. A fourth of the blood supply, at any given moment, is coursing through the brain.[2] Physical activities alter the chemistry of the blood.[3] Whatever affects the chemistry of the bloodstream will have immediate mental consequences.

A BALANCING ACT

Your mental performance state at any given time reflects a delicate chemical balance among assorted hormones and compounds known as neurotransmitters.

Norepinephrine is both a hormone and a neurotransmitter. Without it in your system, you're asleep. Not enough norepinephrine, and you're sluggish and lethargic; you'd make a tree sloth look ambitious. Too much norepinephrine, and you're keyed up and jittery, tensed at the edge and ready to explode. If you've got the right amount, then you're energized and confident, able to perform at the top of your form.

But norepinephrine isn't the only substance that affects your mental state. Your body produces many other chemicals so powerful that minute amounts can change your performance state: acetylcholine, dopamine, epinephrine, serotonin, the endorphins, and others.

Every day, millions of Americans adjust their chemical balance with drugs—legal substances like caffeine and alcohol, or prescription pharmaceuticals like amphetamines and barbiturates. Many risk prison, poisoning, and poverty by developing a taste for cocaine, heroin, or both.

These drugs function by changing the chemical balance in the bloodstream. Cocaine, for instance, increases the body's production of norepinephrine. A line or two energizes mind and body; a little more leads to frazzled nerves.[4] Heroin and its opiate relatives are merely chemical cousins of substances that the body produces anyway—the endorphins. Through the network of the nervous system, the natural endorphins work the same way as the opiate drugs. The shape of the molecules is such that they fit into the same places on nerve cells as the neurotransmitters that convey pain signals. So the endorphins and the opiates block the transmission of pain signals from the body to the brain. Inside the limbic system, by a mechanism still not fully understood, they stimulate the pleasure centers.[5]

To provide energy without tension and put yourself in the Ideal Performance State, you could cook up some speedballs (a mixture of cocaine and heroin) and inject them. If your timing and dosage were perfect, you'd be at the top of your abilities—for a few minutes.

That's one of the problems: These exotic external substances wear off quickly. Then there's the expense, as well as the aggravation and nuisance of maintaining a supply in the face of opposition from the police department. Other complications include adulterants and lethal overdoses.

Getting into the Ideal Performance State does not require poppy juice or tropical leaf extract. Plain old physical exercise does a better job of adjusting the chemical balance in your nervous system. It functions as a stimulant because it increases your norepinephrine levels. Even though you are being stimulated, you do not become nervous and edgy.

When you exercise, your body produces more endorphins, the built-in "opiates" that reduce pain, enhance pleasure, and make you feel relaxed.[6]

Knowing how and when to exercise is like owning an inexhaustible stock of powerful yet safe mood-altering drugs. The drugs and their effects are always under your control because they're part of the standard equipment that comes with every human nervous system.

Motion controls emotion.

PHYSICAL PERFORMANCE AND INTERNAL ENERGY STATES

High Intensity

HIGH POSITIVE	HIGH NEGATIVE
Energy without tension	*Tension with energy*
Calm, but energized; response, engaged. Coordinated and graceful, actions appropriate to situation.	Tense, edgy; movements jerky and difficult to control. Coordination of fine muscles suffers and responses often totally inappropriate.

Pleasant _____ **Unpleasant**

LOW POSITIVE	LOW NEGATIVE
Neither energy nor tension	*Tension without energy*
Relaxed, lethargic, unperturbed, open and at ease. Relaxed.	Stiff, slow, halting responses; poor coordination.

Low Intensity

DISARMING THE HIGH NEGATIVE

Many daily challenges push you toward the High Negative. You're working on something and it doesn't seem to be going right. That's frustrating enough, but the distractions and other demands start to mount. You can't find enough time to do it right so you keep doing it over. Anger, frustration, and tension build and build some more.

How do you release the tension? A few shots of Scotch, perhaps a Valium? But with those you will be hazy for a few hours; you need to stay focused.

There's the traditional physical response: Hit something, throw something, or kick something. That releases the tension so that you can focus on the challenge—often, alas, some new challenges. Like learning to type with one hand because your other is throbbing after you tried to teach the reluctant keyboard a lesson. Or finding your only 12-mm offset end wrench after you heaved it across the shop. Or finding a new job—you had to kick something, didn't you, and how were you to know the boss would be standing on the other side of the shattered water cooler?

As nervous tension builds, it is reflected in increased muscular tension. Releasing one kind of tension will release the other. For a controlled release, try one of these:

The Enhanced Shrug

This works best if you stand, but you can do it while sitting.

Clench your fists and tense your arms and legs. Jerk your shoulders as high as they will go. Hold this awful position for ten to fifteen seconds.

Close your eyes and imagine that massive leaden weights have been placed atop your shoulders. The only way to release the burden is to let the weights slide down, through your arms and legs, as you slowly drop your shoulders.

Repeat three or four times; the High Negative tension will vanish, but your energy and intensity will remain.

Putting On the Squeeze

Push your chair back from your desk and cross your arms around your chest. Begin to squeeze all the air you can from your lungs. Squeeze hard. As you push more and more air from your lungs, bend forward at the waist, and squeeze to a count of eight.

Now relax your arms and upper body, start to inhale, and gradually extend your arms upward and outward toward your head. As you extend them farther and farther, take in air until your lungs are full. Reach as far as you can with your outstretched arms as if gathering energy from the universe and drawing it into you, to a count of eight.

Repeat the cycle three times.

Desk Isometrics

Performing isometric exercises while at your desk is easy: Push downward, upward, and outward with your arms and hands from various positions around your desk and chair. If your chair is stable and has strong armrests, you can lift yourself up and down from your seat. If the chair isn't stable, you can push isometrically on the arms, and get much the same benefit. To relax tension in the lower body, perform leg lifts while sitting, or push against the inside of your desk with your legs.

PUMPING INTENSITY

Often it is difficult to get into a task. Your task, along with its premature deadline, sits right there in front of you. And you just sit there, too. You feel fine, but you can't seem to get going. Your attention wanders from football to fashion and you're about as intense as a marshmallow.

That means that it's time to take a break. Not a coffee break, but an exercise break.

In many productive Japanese companies, exercise breaks are scheduled and organized. The entire assembly line stops for fifteen minutes as the workers step back and perform calisthenics in unison.[7] Our culture is more individualistic; we doubt that any program so structured would go over well in American society.

Fortunately, you benefit just as much from a solo exercise break.

A few minutes of vigorous activity stimulates norepinephrine production, thus making you more alert and energized. At the same time, serotonin and endorphin levels rise, insuring that tension does not rise.

Further, the exercise makes you breathe more deeply as your heart pumps more blood. Thus the brain receives more energy. These exercises also involve both sides of your body—which means that both halves of your brain are stimulated as they control the physical activities. This leads to the full use of your mental powers when you return to the task.[8]

Here are some good office pick-me-ups to use during those times of day when you find yourself running out of steam. Morning people often hit a three o'clock slump every afternoon, while night people might want to try these energizers at the start of the workday.

Rope Jumping with an Imaginary Rope

Pretend you have a rope, and go for it with both arms and legs, for two to five minutes. Jump on your toes but make as little noise as possible with your feet. Make it more fun by getting fancy—double jumps, triple jumps, alternate feet, slow motion, etc.

Quick Calisthenics

—*Bent-knee sit-ups.* Fifty to a hundred of these will enhance your circulation and deepen your breathing so that you can return to your task with more energy. The long-term results—stronger abdominal muscles and a flatter belly—will please you, too.

—*Muscle stretching.* As personal computers and video display terminals arrived in offices, so did aching necks and backs. To reduce these aches, develop a routine that stretches all your major muscle groups: Extend your arms and twist them, touch your toes, stand on one foot and stretch the other leg, bend your head back, and so forth. Experiment until you find a five- to ten-minute routine that gets rid of these aches.

—*Eye relaxers.* Many personal (as opposed to organizational) headaches associated with computerization come from eyestrain. Keeping the eyes focused continually on a close object requires precise muscular control, and those muscles become fatigued. You can relax them during your exercise break by shifting your visual focus to distant objects.

Getting On and Off the Treadmill

If your work at your desk makes you feel as though you are on a treadmill, going as hard as you can but getting nowhere, then it's time to pretend you're really on a treadmill.

Get up and run in place for five to ten minutes. You will return to your task with improved concentration and alertness. Running in place is also a great way to stimulate creative problem-solving when you're stuck.

MORE THAN A MINUTE

Physical exercise is a practical short-term tactic for controlling your performance state. It's safer and cheaper than any drug known to pharmaceutical science; it's powerful, and the improved mental performance shows up almost instantly. Over the long term, exercise can do even more.

Like it or not, you live in a society that often makes judgments on the basis of reasons that seem irrelevant.

The rules of formal logic assert that the validity of a statement has nothing to do with its source. But it seldom works that way in the Real World. If a suggestion, question, order, or the like comes from someone who's shy and halting, who's slouched and panting and nervous, whose clothes don't fit—what happens? Generally nothing. But if it comes from someone who's standing straight and serene, whose appearance radiates confidence, then things happen.

Good body tone thus enhances self-confidence. People are understandably more likely to believe in you and your work if you exhibit a belief in yourself and your skills.

The workouts that shrink flabby bellies also build confidence. When you trust your appearance and don't have to worry about any poor impression that it might make, you are free to concentrate on your performance. Your performances improve.

Further, the process of building your body tone requires a succession of incremental steps. You set goals and meet them for an extended period; you feel better about yourself and your abilities. That builds confidence faster than it builds muscles.

The ultimate confidence of mental toughness comes from developing the stamina to meet the sustained challenges.

FOOD FOR THOUGHT

Nerve cells differ from muscle cells in many respects, but both get their energy from the same source—the glucose and oxygen carried in the blood.

The oxygen comes from respiration. As blood courses through the lungs, the hemoglobin in the red blood cells picks up oxygen molecules inhaled from the atmosphere. Glucose is a simple sugar; the body can produce it from all manner of foods. When the two are combined, energy is given off, just as energy results from the combustion of gasoline and oxygen in the cylinders of an automobile engine. The body's tricarboxylic acid cycle is much more complicated than what happens in engines, but the result is the same: Through combustion, glucose and oxygen become physical energy.[9]

They also represent mental energy, since the brain requires such tremendous quantities of glucose and oxygen. Ample supplies of both must be available if the brain is to perform at its best. If your body is not processing enough glucose and oxygen, you'll feel it when you try to move, and you'll also notice it when you try to think.

"Hypoxia" is the medical term for a lack of oxygen; in mountainous regions, it's called "altitude sickness." It has physical symptoms, known to any climber who gets much higher than 10,000 feet above sea level without an adjustment period. In those circumstances, it's hard to make the legs move; when they do, it is without grace or precision. The mental symptoms include light-headedness, difficulty in concentrating, and loss of comprehension. Clear thinking is impossible without enough oxygen.[10]

When the blood does not supply enough glucose, the result is hypoglycemia, with similar mental disruption: loss of alertness, drowsiness, headache.[11]

When you suffer from mental exhaustion after a prolonged bout of concentration, how do you feel? It's hard to focus. You miss much of what's going on around you. You feel drowsy and your head hurts. Your energy supplies are depleted; your mind can't function properly because it isn't getting enough fuel. Your performance suffers until you can restore the supply through rest.

That's fine if you've got time for a break just then. But the world has an annoying habit of throwing challenges at us whether we're rested or not. The only way to guarantee readiness is to build up a reservoir of energy that can be drawn upon as necessary.

ENLARGING THE SUPPLY

There is a way to enlarge the supply of both essential mental fuels. It is known as aerobic exercise.

The bodily blessings of aerobic exercise attract new converts every day. But we want to focus on the cerebral benefits. Aerobic exercise builds mental stamina, be it for a grueling and extended chess match, sustained concentration upon craftsmanship, or intelligent decision-making all day, every day.

"Aerobic" means "with air." Aerobic exercise is exercise that makes you breathe deeply on a consistent basis for extended periods. As you do that, your heart pumps more blood, and your body responds to the increased physical demands by:[12]

1. Making more red blood cells. The average person has about 5 million of them in a cubic milliliter. Someone who has been in a good aerobic program carries close to 8 million. Red blood cells bring oxygen to the brain; the more of them, the more oxygen there is, and the more effectively the nervous system can function.

2. Improving respiratory efficiency. Air generally contains 21 percent oxygen when you inhale and 19 percent when you exhale. But the lungs of an aerobic exerciser work more efficiently; only 17 percent of an exhalation is oxygen. The lungs have become twice as efficient. The result, again, is more oxygen and improved mental performance.

3. Providing more glucose. The body does not store glucose. As you eat, you take what you need from the small intestine, and the other glucose goes to the liver, where it is stored as glycogen, a starch. Between digestions, the liver converts glycogen into glucose—but at a fairly steady rate in keeping with the body's usual demands.[13]

   If more energy is needed in a hurry, as when a challenge presents itself, it is impossible for the liver to speed up in time. To provide the energy, the body releases epinephrine (adrenaline), which among other things breaks down glycogen into glucose. Nerve cells and muscle cells get more energy, but at the price of having epinephrine pumped into the system.

   Aerobic exercise raises the body's habitual glucose demand; the steady flow of energy rises. The brain can get fuel without becoming alarmed; you can think your way through a challenge without falling victim to the "fight or flight" stress reaction.

Now it is clear why Bobby Fischer trained his body to prepare for a chess match. By building physical stamina through aerobic exercise, he was building the mental stamina of a world champion.

PROGRAM PROBLEMS

If you're one of the millions of Americans involved in a regular aerobic exercise program, that's great.

If you haven't started, it's probably for a good reason. Give us a chance to deal with those reasons.

I hate to run. You probably loved to run when you were little.

Then you encountered a sadistic physical education teacher who used running as punishment: "Hey, punk, I saw you lollygagging there. That'll be eight laps." Or maybe it was a drill instructor who improved the nation's defense by ordering you to double-time for six miles through mud with a full pack.

Those are perfectly good reasons to despise the very thought of running.

Running is the most popular form of aerobic exercise —it doesn't take much in the way of special equipment, and you can do it almost any time in almost any location. But it isn't the only form. Cycling and swimming provide the same benefits, as do cross-country skiing, skipping, or chopping wood, which is President Reagan's favorite exercise.

You don't have to run to have an aerobic program. So if you hate running, don't. Do something else. The links between motion and emotion show up during exercise. Exercise must be enjoyed in a state of fun, or it's a waste of time and a drain of energy.

This is demonstrated in Sweden, in a study of overweight sergeants who had to lose weight to stay in the service.[14] They were split into two groups who had identical diets and exercise routines, mostly running. The only difference was in how they approached their exercises.

One group went at it positively, with support and encouragement from the instructor, who made it fun. The other group was instilled with a sense of drudgery and oppression concerning exercise.

Since both groups took in 1,400 calories a day and expended about 3,000, the results should have been the same. But they weren't. The positive group lost weight twice as quickly as the others. The positive group showed the usual benefits of exercise—increased lung capacity, higher red blood cell count, etc. The negative group showed almost imperceptible improvements; the exercise hardly benefited them at all.

If you don't enjoy your workout, you will shortchange yourself of the benefits of exercise.

I've got bad knees, and running is too hard on them. I don't want to cripple myself. Who does want to cripple himself?

Running is hard on knees and ankles; it causes more injuries to those joints than all the other forms of exercise put together.[15] Not everyone is built to stand up to the pounding.

Swimming or cycling provides the same aerobic benefits without stressing those vulnerable joints.

Dr. Irv Dardik, former head of the United States Olympic Council on Sports Medicine, suggests skipping. It puts less stress on vulnerable joints, and it provides that all-important state of fun.[16]

I'm really busy. I don't have the time to get into all those hours of exercise. Lots of people really do get into aerobics; some fanatics devote three or four hours a day.

On that level, aerobic exercise is a healthful hobby. However, it doesn't require anywhere near that amount of time to build mental stamina.

To increase your brain's fuel supply, you need to engage

in aerobic exercise for about thirty minutes a day, four times a week. More exercise won't hurt, but this minimum will improve your body's ability to provide energy to the mind.[17]

You're not looking for the impossible, like finding two or three hours in days that are already jammed. You're looking at two hours a week.

You will regain that two hours and more, thanks to improved performance.

During the past decade, many corporations launched employee fitness programs on financial grounds—healthy employees aren't sick as often. That boosts productivity right there, and it also means a reduction in health-insurance premiums, a major cost of business.

But the companies found that fitness also paid off in increased day-to-day productivity. Fit people get more done in an hour than unfit people do. And they were not shoveling coal or otherwise deploying their muscles; they were processing insurance claims or writing computer software. Productivity gains of 20 percent are not uncommon.[18]

Suppose your career demands sixty hours a week. In theory, devoting two of those hours to aerobic exercise would decrease your production by 3.33 percent. But your enhanced mental stamina and energy level mean that you'll be doing as much in fifty hours as you did before in sixty hours. You gain eight hours.

I always push myself too hard. If I exercised, I'd probably push myself right into a heart attack. We've seen what happens when you do exercise. You're on the track, strained and grunting and wheezing, gritting your teeth, making sure you go a kilometer farther than everybody else. It proves something. Even in a friendly game, you take tennis more seriously than Jimmy Connors does.

Exercising under these conditions is hard on your heart; such exercise does not decrease the risk of coronary problems.

You're a competitive person. You're driven. But compete only in your chosen arena. Making exercise into a demonstration of who's best is like going out to lunch and demonstrating that you're the top performer because you can eat more food than anyone else at the table.

If you're a Type A person, you still need the benefits of aerobic exercise. But you'll have to go about it more cautiously. Consult your physician. Learn how to monitor your heartbeat to keep it within a safe range; you might want to investigate a device like the Quantum XL Heart Monitor, which sends an alarm if your heartbeat is too rapid.

It hurts to exercise. It certainly does hurt to exercise if you start at it in the wrong way. Pain is your body's way of telling you that something has gone wrong.

The most common problem comes the first day. You set off jogging, cycling, swimming, or even briskly walking. A few minutes later, your thighs are coiled up like watchsprings and you didn't know it was possible to hurt that much. If you're persistent, then you keep trying, hoping that you will get used to it. But it is a lot like getting used to sitting on a hot stove. You're not a masochist, so you give up on exercise.

Paying off accrued debts is a painful process, and the pain means that you're paying off an oxygen debt. When you began to move quickly, you increased the body's demand for glucose and oxygen. Normally, your muscles take in glucose and oxygen and expel carbon dioxide, which is carried off by the blood.

But with a greater demand, the body cannot respond quickly enough with supplies from the normal sources. There just isn't enough oxygen, so the muscles start to get energy from glucose through fermentation, instead of combustion.

The blood cannot carry off the resulting waste product, lactic acid. It builds up in the muscles and it hurts like hell. Eventually you stop moving and start gasping for breath, so that the oxygen can reach the muscles and convert the lactic acid into something that the blood can haul away.[19]

Increasing your energy supply through aerobic exercise is a gradual process. Start slowly. If muscle cramps develop, you're going too fast. A good rule is to stay at a pace that allows you to converse. With time, that pace will speed up.

Exercise at the proper pace produces not pain, but pleasure. It stimulates the body's production of endorphins, those natural opiates that block pain and produce pleasure in the brain centers that control emotion.

I've tried, but I have trouble sticking to an exercise program. In many demanding careers, it's impossible to build in a daily exercise session at 5 P.M. Your schedule is erratic, or you're on the road most of the time. You aren't always in control of your schedule, and that makes it difficult to get into an exercise routine.

Focus on what you can control.

The most certain way to insure that you get exercise is to build it into your life. Instead of driving, bicycle, jog, or walk briskly to the office. Use the stairs (seven or eight stories at a steady pace is a pretty good aerobic workout) instead of riding the elevator. When you're on the road, swim in the motel pool. Look for opportunities to exercise, and take advantage of them.

I already exercise. I lift weights and I play some golf. I'm fairly trim. Why should I join this aerobics craze? Every form of exercise offers benefits. Golf, tennis, volleyball, softball, and the like are fun, and give you a chance to socialize while relaxing. They enhance your muscle tone, coordination, and confidence. But they don't require sustained deep breathing, so such exercises do not build mental stamina in any consistent way.

Calisthenics, weight lifting, and the other programs offered in fitness centers will improve your appearance, agility, body tone, strength, and confidence. But they are seldom done in an aerobic manner, and won't help you build the energy reserves required for sustained performance.

An aerobic exercise program—running, cycling, or

swimming—is the only way to improve the brain's fuel supply. And it also offers most of the other benefits of exercise: relaxation, better appearance, improved body tone, confidence.

It comes down to a question of maximizing the return on the time and effort you invest. The benefit-cost ratio is greatest with an aerobic program that involves at least half an hour of sustained deep breathing, four times a week. If you have more time for exercise—and we hope you do—then you can invest that time in more aerobics, or in golf or tennis or weight lifting, and gain even more benefits. But aerobics must be the foundation of your exercise program if you want to develop the stamina of mental toughness.

DESIGNING YOUR PROGRAM

1. Create a playframe around every part of your program. Make it a point to have fun during each phase.
2. If you're over thirty-five, or have a history of heart problems, knee injuries, or similar ailments, see your physician first.
3. Start slowly. The "no pain–no gain" formula does not apply here. Your workouts should last at least thirty minutes, but should not be painful. Establish aerobic target heart rates and keep yourself within the target zone. To find your target heart rate, subtract your age from 220, and multiply that figure by .80. Consult any current exercise book if you need more information.
4. Don't overdo. You should be able to carry on a normal conversation while exercising. You should feel little or no pain, and your breathing should be regular and comfortable. If any of these is not true, *slow down*.
5. Keep an accurate record of your efforts, especially the effect that your exercise program has on your energy levels, mood states, stress levels, attitude, and overall performance levels. The following chart is one way to track these important relationships.

EXERCISE–MENTAL TOUGHNESS MONITORING CHART
Effects of Exercise on Internal Energy State Control

Date								
Time								
Intensity (H/M/L)								
Was it fun? (Y/N)								
Energy level 1 hour later (H/M/L)								
Energy level 3 hours later (H/M/L)								
Mood after workout (A–F)								
Stress level after workout (H/M/L)								
Attitude after workout (A–F)								
How well I performed today (A–F)								

H–High   M–Medium   L–Low
A–Excellent   B–Good   C–Average   D–Poor   F–Very Poor

7
DIET:
The Mood and Food Connection

IDEAL PERFORMANCE STATE: MOOD CONTROL

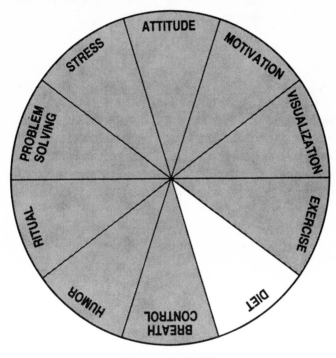

STRATEGIES

There is a direct relationship between diet and mental performance.

Modify your dietary habits and you can achieve substantially greater emotional control.

Sustained mental energy results from eating the right foods at the right times.

What you eat, how much you eat, and when you eat it change not only the chemistry of your digestive tract, but also the chemical balance of your nervous system. Your emotional state, and consequently your mood and your ability to perform, is a direct reflection of that delicate chemical balance in the brain. The major difference between food and drugs, in this respect, is that you ingest more food.

For generations, scientists maintained that food was merely fuel. Food was related to brains about as closely as coal was related to computers. The power plant burns the coal to make steam which spins turbines to produce a flow of electrons which eventually moves through logic gates. The nature of the fuel concerned the power company, but not the computer, which ran just the same whether they were burning peat moss, mill scraps, or anthracite in the distant boilers.

In the body, this theory held that all food was broken down to maintain stable chemical concentrations throughout the brain and body. Protected by a membrane called "the blood-brain barrier," the mind grabbed whatever nutrients and chemicals it needed from the bloodstream.[1] Some potent drugs were able to penetrate this barrier, but not everyday food, which had no effect on mental functioning. There were appetite signals, but that was the extent of the link between food and mood. As long as there were no hunger pangs and cravings, the emotional centers of the brain didn't care whether the body was digesting glazed doughnuts, porterhouse steak, or brown rice.

And that was about as wrong as a theory can get.

About a decade ago, Dr. Richard Wurtman of the Massachusetts Institute of Technology made an important discovery: The levels of serotonin in the brain are a direct result of the amount of tryptophan in the bloodstream. Serotonin, one of about thirty neurotransmitters, conveys impulses between nerve cells in the brain centers responsible for pleasure and relaxation. The more serotonin, the more of those feelings. Tryptophan, an amino acid, is present in many foods, and the body uses it to make serotonin. When the blood contains more tryptophan, the brain makes more serotonin.[2]

Your emotional state and consequent mental performance reflect the chemical balance in your brain. How well you perform at a 10:00 A.M. presentation is a result of your emotional state—your brain's chemical balance. It is now established that this chemical balance is affected by your breakfast menu.

A breakfast rich in carbohydrates (juice, toast, and jelly, for example) leads to a higher serotonin level than does a breakfast rich in protein (milk, bacon, and eggs). The higher serotonin level means you're less likely to feel depressed or tense, which means you're more likely to perform well. But if the serotonin level goes too high, you'll be sleepy.

Similar links have been established between tyrosine, a compound present in many foods, and norepinephrine, a neurotransmitter that stimulates mental processes as well as pulse and respiration.

CHEMICAL MOODS

The components of specific foods can cause measurable changes in your internal chemistry. Since most foods are quite complex—made out of many components—the relationship between food and mood has been difficult to quantify. Enough has been learned, however, to gain a basic understanding.

By adjusting your diet, you can insure that you will have adequate levels of tryptophan and tyrosine, thus guaranteeing that the chemical components of the High Positive will be available to your nervous system.

However, it is not as simple as finding foods that are rich in tryptophan and tyrosine.

SIMPLIFIED RELATIONSHIP
OF
INTERNAL ENERGY STATES,
NEUROTRANSMITTERS,
AND AMINO ACIDS

High Intensity

HIGH POSITIVE	**HIGH NEGATIVE**
Energy without tension	*Tension with energy*
Neurotransmitters:	Neurotransmitter:
Norepinephrine and serotonin in balance.	Epinephrine; the level varies with the quantity of tyrosine.

Pleasant _____ **Unpleasant**

LOW POSITIVE	**LOW NEGATIVE**
Neither energy nor tension	*Tension without energy*
Neurotransmitter:	Neurotransmitter:
Serotonin; the level varies with the amount of tryptophan.	Deficient levels of both norepinephrine and serotonin.

Low Intensity

Tryptophan is a protein, one of the twenty-two amino acids that the body uses as building blocks for growth and repair. Although tryptophan is the scarcest of the amino acids, any food rich in protein will contain tryptophan. But a protein diet paradoxically does not increase the amount of tryptophan that reaches the brain. Tryptophan, it turns out, has a hard time getting into the brain when other proteins are present in the bloodstream.

Eating carbohydrates forces the body to produce insulin, which chases most other proteins out of the bloodstream. This increases the amount of tryptophan in proportion to other proteins in the blood, and thus increases its chance of getting into the brain.

To maximize tryptophan in the bloodstream, the best results known to date have come from about two ounces of carbohydrates on an empty stomach.[3] If you want to drift off to sleep, or you feel tense and edgy, eat a muffin or a couple of crackers. Your serotonin levels will rise in about thirty minutes, and you will feel more relaxed and pleasant.

Conversely, if you feel sluggish but positive, try a food rich in protein, and your serotonin level generally drops. Because milk is rich in protein, the traditional bedtime glass of milk seldom provides its anticipated relaxation.

Tryptophan always increases serotonin production, but that isn't so with tyrosine and norepinephrine. Tyrosine, another amino acid present in many foods, increases norepinephrine production only when the nervous systems that use norepinephrine are already active and firing. And science has yet to discover a dietary method of increasing tyrosine levels. No foods are especially rich in tyrosine, and there isn't any method of eating that will remove its protein competitors from the bloodstream.

The key to adequate levels of both, as well as the other nutrients the brain and body require, lies in a balanced and varied diet, and in avoiding foods that are known to depress performance.

THE NONPERFORMANCE DIET

The diet that is all too typical among American performers goes something like this:

Skip breakfast; there isn't time.
Once the hunger pangs start going strong, usually about 10 A.M., chomp on something—maybe a chocolate-covered doughnut.
At lunch, enjoy a couple of drinks, along with a steak sandwich and french fries. And maybe some salad for the health of it, but smother it with an oily dressing.
Coffee and a candy bar at 3 P.M.

Big dinner at 7 P.M., after a couple of drinks.
Some brownies and milk at bedtime, or maybe chips and
dip during the late show.

If you really tried, you could probably come up with a
more defeating diet. But it would be difficult. Skipping
breakfast, snacking on junk foods, taking in too many proteins and fats, and indulging in big meals are ways to insure
that mental toughness is a sporadic accident, rather than
a consistent performance.

Consistent high-quality mental performance is the result
of a consistent high-quality energy supply.

A LOOK AT NUTRITION

Food contains six basic and required nutrients: water,
minerals, vitamins, proteins, fat, and carbohydrates.[4]

The body manages water pretty well through thirst,
urination, and perspiration; it's seldom a concern. Although vitamins and minerals are necessities of life, some
vitamins and minerals are present in virtually everything
you eat, and your diet, if it is at all varied, will provide
sufficient quantities of vitamins and minerals. Rarely is
there a problem with these that would affect your performance.

However, the amount, quality, and timing of proteins,
fat, and carbohydrates have a direct effect on mental performance, thanks to the way the digestive system works to
provide fuel for mind and body.

In many respects, nerve cells function differently from
muscle cells. But they both get their energy from the same
two substances—glucose and oxygen, carried by the blood.

Glucose is a simple sugar; when it unites with oxygen
in a process similar to burning, the result is energy. Glucose
is present in some foods, and the body is quite efficient at
converting carbohydrates into glucose. If necessary, the
body can also convert proteins and fat into glucose.

If there isn't enough glucose in the bloodstream, the result is hypoglycemia. Its symptoms include drowsiness, fatigue, headache, nervousness, and depression; it is obviously impossible to be in the Ideal Performance State while suffering from hypoglycemia.[5]

On the other hand, it isn't a good thing to have too much glucose in the bloodstream, either. Corn syrup is nearly pure glucose; it's thick. As the glucose concentration rises, the blood thickens, and that means more work for the heart in pumping the blood through an estimated 60,000 miles of tiny vessels.[6] That's no ticket to top performance, either.

So the body tries to maintain an appropriate glucose level, providing more when energy demands are high, and cutting back while resting.

THROUGH THE DAY

With that in mind, let's look at how the Nonperformance Diet works against you.

When you awaken, it is after a period of low energy demand. The body does not store glucose; whatever is not consumed immediately is converted to glycogen and stored in the liver, to be released and converted back to glucose as necessary. During the night, this process was understandably running at a slow pace.

Your energy demands rise when you do, but it takes time for the complex chemistry to adjust. If you eat breakfast right away, your brain and body will start getting their glucose from the food as it is digested.

Since you don't, the liver dumps a lot of glycogen into the system to be converted to glucose. The quick way to do that is by pumping in some epinephrine (adrenaline), which speeds up the conversion of glycogen into glucose. It also speeds your pulse, makes you breathe shallowly, and builds nervous tension, putting you into the High Negative.

By mid-morning, your blood-sugar level has dropped again, which triggers the appestat (a nervous center that controls appetite) in the brain's limbic system, the same neural center that controls emotion. So you feel hungry and grab a chocolate-covered doughnut.

Chocolate may be a socially acceptable addiction, but it's not much help to a performing nervous system. As the chocolate is metabolized, it becomes phenylalanine, another neurotransmitter. High phenylalanine levels have been linked to depression, lethargy, and anxiety.[7]

But there is plenty of sugar on and in that doughnut, isn't there? And sugar means energy, doesn't it?

Common sugar is sucrose; chemically, it is merely two glucose molecules jammed together. As soon as it gets into the body, it breaks apart and dissolves into the bloodstream—so that ought to produce a quick rise in the amount of fuel for the nervous system.

But it doesn't. Remember that glucose levels can't rise too high, or the blood would be too thick. To make sure that doesn't happen, the pancreas secretes the hormone insulin whenever the glucose level rises quickly. Insulin speeds the conversion of glucose into glycogen. It also changes the cell walls, so that they will absorb glucose more rapidly. The level of glucose quickly drops.

Insulin works only on muscle cells, though. That's why you feel a physical rush after eating sugar. Insulin doesn't affect the nerve cells—they don't get to partake of this glucose feast. To recap, sugar makes the glucose level rise, which brings on the insulin. The muscles get more energy, but the brain doesn't. And when the glucose level drops as a result of the insulin, there's just that much less fuel for the brain.[8]

Your body feels energized for a few minutes after the doughnut. Then your glucose level drops, and your performance reflects it—you're tired, nervous, and depressed. All sugar does is starve your brain. It's as if you started a fire next to your desk because you wanted to be warm. But just as soon as you began to feel the heat, the fire set off the sprinkler system, and you ended up cold and doused.

But you make it through the morning and go to lunch. The hamburger is full of protein—and fat. It's more of both than you need.

The body extracts the necessary protein and fat. If your ongoing energy demands are high, it can convert the protein and fat into glycogen and glucose. Otherwise, the protein becomes fat, and it joins the other fat in storage.

Making all these transformations requires energy that you might have applied to something else.

To draw an analogy, consider a high-performance car like a Ferrari. It runs on high-octane fuel. But it might be that you're uncertain of the fuel supply, and you want to make sure you'll always be able to drive. So you build a trailer, and on that trailer, you assemble some chemical conversion plants that can transform charcoal, wood scraps, grass clippings, cow manure, and anything else vaguely organic into fuel for the Ferrari. Thus you're always able to drive the Ferrari, but its performance will understandably suffer as it has to haul the trailer behind it and provide the energy required to convert scraps into gasoline. Eating the wrong foods forces your body to do essentially the same thing.

Your body's routine tasks—breathing, digestion, and so forth—are generally controlled by a part of your central nervous system called the autonomic nervous system. The autonomic system has two networks: the parasympathetic nervous system and the sympathetic nervous system.

The parasympathetic system is in charge when you're relaxed and proceeding normally; you breathe slowly and the food progresses through your digestive tract as the nutrients are extracted, right on schedule. When you're alarmed or excited, however, the sympathetic side takes over. You go into the "flight or fight" stage. Your breathing becomes shallow and rapid and your pupils dilate. Because your limbs may require all the energy you can provide them, blood is rushed to them. Digestion stops because the process requires ample supplies of blood, and that blood has been shifted to energize your limbs.

While a heavy meal is being digested, the parasympathetic portion of the body's autonomic nervous system is in charge; your central nervous system is full of serotonin but lacking in norepinephrine—you feel lethargic and sleepy.

And if you must perform while you're running an internal chemical conversion plant, the sympathetic nervous system takes over, pumping out norepinephrine. You're certainly alert and focused and energized, but digestion is interrupted, which leads later to everything from vague pains to wrenching nausea.[9]

Besides that, there was the alcohol in the drinks. Alcohol depresses the central nervous system. It relaxes and eases inhibitions; in controlled amounts, alcohol can be useful for relaxation. But it isn't a performance fuel for humans.

This day was a lucky day—no one expected you to do much after lunch. Which was good, because you sure had trouble maintaining your concentration. Even after that candy bar at three o'clock.

At dinner, you put your body through the lunch ordeal again. The meal is heavy on proteins and fats, so there's no chance that it will raise your tryptophan levels; instead you feel anxious and tense. The sweet dessert doesn't help, either. And the bedtime snack had too much protein; the result was no relaxing serotonin. Since your energy demands were minimal as it was digested, the snack got converted into fat.

Maintaining your weight is a constant struggle, and so is performing in your career. At least it isn't a mystery why this is happening. During the eight hours that you had set aside for your performance, you had your body working against your nervous system. Glucose levels were generally too low. When they were high enough, your neurotransmitters were conspiring to keep you lazy and relaxed. Not that there's anything wrong with that, but it isn't where you perform well.

Use your diet to enhance your performance, instead of letting your diet undermine your performance.

A DESIGNER DIET

Given that the common eating regimen makes top performance difficult, is there one diet which we can recommend that will maximize mental performance?

No.

Everyone functions differently. Consider milk, often promoted as nature's perfect food. It contains many useful nutrients and many people like it. But it also makes many people ill, because their bodies lack an enzyme required for digesting milk.

And there are allergies, which come uncomfortably close to being the least understood phenomenon in medicine. Any specific diet may work for multitudes of people, but may contain something that you're allergic to. Those allergies don't necessarily result in nausea, fever, or chills; many merely lead to headaches, anxiety, insomnia, and irritability—all symptoms that could have other causes.

Further, energy demands vary with individual metabolism.

In short, it is impossible for us or anyone else to publish a diet and assure you that if you follow it, your performance will improve. We can show you an example, and we can give you the guidelines for a performance diet. Then it is possible for you to design your own by paying attention to the kinds of food you eat, the amount you eat, when you eat, and the resulting effects on your performance. In essence, you'll be running a nutrition laboratory wherein you are also the subject of the experiment. You can vary your diet, and see how each variation affects your emotional state and thus your performance. The result will be a maximum-performance diet that works for you.

GRAZE, DON'T GORGE

The most important single purpose of a performance diet is to insure that the nervous system has an adequate and continuous supply of glucose throughout the day. Without that supply, you develop the symptoms of mental fatigue, and sustained concentration is impossible.

Glucose comes from two sources in the body. It can be released from the glycogen stored in the liver. This system is for emergencies, when energy demands rise quickly. That's why the process also requires epinephrine (adrenaline). It isn't efficient, and it wears on the heart.

The other source occurs during digestion. Food passes from the stomach into the intestines, where blood picks up nutrients directly. During heavy digestion, there's too much glucose coming out of the intestine, and the body is busy converting it to glycogen while releasing insulin— which eventually deprives the nervous system of fuel. If digestion is occurring slowly and continuously, though, then the body produces glucose at the proper levels for good mental performance.

That doesn't happen with three big meals a day. But it does occur with small meals at regular intervals, about three hours apart—a style of eating that has come to be known as "grazing."[10]

It also means that food should be eaten slowly. Leisurely dining improves digestive efficiency while reducing the tendency to overeat. If you eat too quickly, the requisite amount of food may be in the stomach, but the nutrients haven't begun to enter the bloodstream; thus, the appetite control centers in the brain assume that you still need food. You're still hungry, so you keep eating even though you've already taken in what you need. Slow it down, and everything stays in sync.

GOOD GRAZING

Two factors determine just how much grazing will improve performance: quantity and quality.

As for quantity, this is as good a time as any to consider calories. A calorie is a measurement of heat energy. As you go through the day, you expend energy that you acquired from food.

If you burn more calories than you took in from food that day, the body makes up the deficit from its reserves —fat. If you burn fewer calories than you ate, the body thriftily stores the surplus calories as fat. The average woman requires about 2,000 calories each day, and the average man, being somewhat larger, requires more—about 2,200 calories.[11]

But those are averages; the actual amount each person uses is determined by physical effort, mental effort, overall metabolism, and a host of other factors. For that reason, we do not recommend that you pay close attention to your caloric intake and expenditure as a means of controlling weight. Instead, get your information from your appearance and your clothes. They'll tell you whether you're losing or gaining weight, and you can adjust your diet accordingly.

Given an average demand of 2,000 to 2,200 calories per day, and the performance diet that involves five small but equal meals, then each meal should contain about 400 calories.

Timing alone will not assure the major benefit of grazing—a steady glucose flow. The body operates its own "chemical plant" to break down complex natural carbohydrates into simple starches and sugars. When the processing has been done before you eat the food, as is the case with refined carbohydrates like sugar, then the resulting glucose goes into the bloodstream much more quickly. This rapid rise in your glucose level means the liver must produce glycogen, and it forces the pancreas to release insulin, which actually works to reduce the flow of energy to the brain.

Complex carbohydrates, such as whole grains and fresh fruits and vegetables, are digested more slowly—in three hours, as opposed to less than an hour for the refined carbohydrates. This slow process means a steadier glucose flow for better mental energy and stamina.[12]

Food is more than carbohydrates and calories; it's also your only source of protein, vitamins, and minerals.

Proteins are building blocks; just about every part of the body is assembled from proteins. Proteins, in turn, are made of simpler chemicals known as amino acids. To make the hundreds of proteins that are as diverse as hair and neurotransmitters, the body requires twenty-two amino acids. Of these twenty-two, all but eight can be made from other substances normally present in the body. If one of the remaining eight is missing, then the body cannot make the proteins it requires. Those eight essential amino acids—tryptophan, leucine, lysine, methionin, phenylalanine, isoleucine, valine, and threonine—must be supplied by your diet. There's no other source.[13]

Meat is predominantly protein; three ounces of meat provide all the protein that an adult requires in a day. Typically, though, the diet provides three or four times that much. The excess has to be converted to fat, a process that consumes energy and keeps you from performing well during digestion. Red meat (beef, veal, mutton, pork) is also rich in fat—which you usually don't need. Fish and fowl carry less fat; they're a far better source of protein.

It is possible to get all the necessary protein from a vegetarian diet, and about 10 million Americans do so, with more joining them every day. If the idea appeals to you, look into it. We don't promote it because constructing a balanced vegetarian diet takes more time and effort than most people are willing to devote.

As for vitamins and minerals, it is virtually impossible not to get adequate amounts of both if you're eating a varied diet. They aren't worth worrying about unless you feel run down and your physician, after proper testing, suggests something like an iron supplement or a vitamin package.

SOME OTHER CONSIDERATIONS

The performance diet, then, consists of small meals of varied complex foods, eaten at intervals of about three hours. Although society seems to be structured for three meals, it isn't that difficult to eat five—every career, even tightly scheduled work on an assembly line, offers morning and afternoon coffee breaks, and that's enough time for a small 400-calorie meal.

Nutritionists, and our own experiences confirm this, advise that the optimum diet should provide about 60 percent of its calories from carbohydrates, 25 percent from fats, and 15 percent from protein.[14]

But how do you balance those meals to insure that you're getting the proper mixture of nutrients? Carry a book around that lists the chemical composition of every known foodstuff, along with some triple-beam scales? Milk has so much protein, and so much fat; vegetables are full of carbohydrates, but they also have protein, and each one is different—is it going to take a huge spreadsheet to figure all this, and then where would you find time to do anything else?

It's simpler than that. For our purposes, foods can be classified according to their major component. Meat and milk, even though they contain other components, can be figured strictly as protein. Vegetables count as carbohydrates, and so forth. As long as you vary your diet, the other factors will average out; this quick method of balancing a diet is surprisingly accurate.[15]

Proteins: Meat and meat products, fish and seafood, milk, buttermilk, yogurt, and cheese.

Fats: Butter, margarine, other fats and oils, mayonnaise, gravies and dressings, peanuts, all nuts, olives, avocados.

Carbohydrates: Fruits, vegetables, bread, rice, potatoes, pasta, cakes, and other desserts.

One day's performance diet, then, might look something like this:

SAMPLE PERFORMANCE DIET

	Calories assigned to:		
TIME AND FOOD	**Carbohydrates**	**Fat**	**Protein**
7:00 A.M.			
2 slices whole-wheat toast	112		
1 tablespoon butter		101	
8 oz. tomato juice	46		
1 banana	105		
Total Breakfast Calories: 364			
10:00 A.M.			
1 apple	81		
2 oz. unsalted corn chips	253		
Total Midmorning Calories: 334			
12:30 P.M.			
Tossed salad:			
1 cup lettuce	10		
1 tomato	33		
3 crackers	40		
1 tablespoon Italian dressing		69	
1/2 avocado		162	
8 oz. skim milk			86
Total Lunch Calories: 400			
3:00 P.M.			
1 orange	62		
1 bran muffin	104		
4 oz. plain yogurt			70
Total Afternoon Calories: 236			
6:30 P.M.			
6 oz. white wine	137		
8 oz. broiled chicken			180
1 whole-wheat roll	90		
1 tablespoon butter		101	
5 oz. steamed asparagus	35		
1 large baked potato	145		
1 oz. sour cream		62	
Total Dinner Calories: 684			
Day's Total Calories: 2,084			
TOTALS	1,253	495	336
Percentages	60.1	23.8	16.1

That's just an example of a diet that meets performance standards. The timing, balance, and calories are good, although it could probably stand fewer refined foods. It might be your diet on one day, but then again, you may find that some chemical present only in bananas makes you feel a bit under the weather. You might not like tomatoes.

That is one of the most important criteria in designing a performance diet for yourself. Your diet must contain foods that you like. Eating agreeable foods is pleasant; even thinking about them causes powerful changes in the nervous system that give you a more positive outlook on everything.[16] Further, a performance diet is not something you follow for two months, until you've adjusted your weight, say, and then abandon. A performance diet is something you follow for the rest of your life, and the pleasures of eating are an important part of your life. A performance diet ought to enhance your life; you must not see it as a deprivation.

YOUR NUTRITION LABORATORY

You're now ready to start your experiments to design your personal performance diet. You should keep a daily chart, for at least a month, of what you eat, when you eat it, and how your diet directly affects your Internal Energy State. Then you'll have one more powerful tool to control your emotional state and enhance your energy.

The following chart is based on the one we use for our workshops and consulting work. Calorie tables are included in many reference books (the *World Almanac*, for instance) and cookbooks.

Feel free to make as many copies of this chart as you need while you perfect your personal performance diet (for your personal use only; not for publication or distribution). Generally, you'll need two charts for each day.

FOOD AND MOOD LOG

Date _____   Page No. _____

Calories of:

TIME	FOOD	QUAN-TITY	CAL-ORIES	Carbo.	Fats	Pro.
____	_____	_____	_____	____	____	____
____	_____	_____	_____	____	____	____
____	_____	_____	_____	____	____	____
____	_____	_____	_____	____	____	____

Energy state
while eating _____ 1 hour later: _____ 2 hours: _____ 3 hours: _____

____	_____	_____	_____	____	____	____
____	_____	_____	_____	____	____	____
____	_____	_____	_____	____	____	____
____	_____	_____	_____	____	____	____

Energy state
while eating _____ 1 hour later: _____ 2 hours: _____ 3 hours: _____

____	_____	_____	_____	____	____	____
____	_____	_____	_____	____	____	____
____	_____	_____	_____	____	____	____
____	_____	_____	_____	____	____	____
____	_____	_____	_____	____	____	____

Energy state
while eating _____ 1 hour later: _____ 2 hours: _____ 3 hours: _____

TOTAL CALORIES   _____ ____ ____ ____
Percentage of calories from:
  Target percentages   60   25   15
                                Carbo. Fats   Pro.

8
BREATH CONTROL:
Riding the Gentle Winds

IDEAL PERFORMANCE STATE: MOOD CONTROL

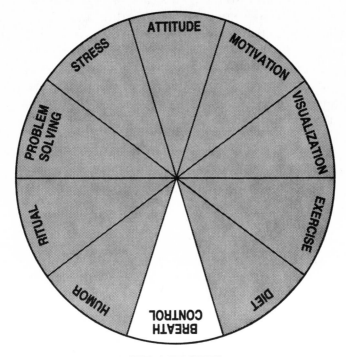

STRATEGIES

Vary breathing techniques to bring calmness and high energy, relaxation, and even better focus.

The biochemistry of emotion and the physiology of breathing unite in the limbic system of the brain.

You can control your emotions by controlling your breath.

"**B**reath's a ware that will not keep," as the poet A. E. Housman noted. The human body cannot store oxygen; the vital gas, which makes up about 20 percent of the atmosphere, must arrive continuously. The body can survive for weeks without eating and days without drinking, but the brain can manage for less than five minutes without oxygen. A quarter of the oxygen in every breath goes to fuel the central nervous system.[1] Breathing is the most direct and most intimate connection from the external world, the world that human beings must perform in, to the inside of the body and the power of the human brain.

The first act that we, as human beings, perform in this world is to breathe; a baby's first breath often follows several hours of the mother's carefully coached inhaling and exhaling.

Since the beginning of language, breath has been synonymous with life itself. The Latin words *spiritus* and *anima*, the Greek *pneuma*, the Hindic *pranayma*, and the Hebrew *nephesh* and *ruakh* all meant not only breath, but the essence of life as well: "And the Lord God formed man of the dust of the ground, and breathed into his nostrils the breath of life; and man became a living soul."[2]

A baby's first breath will be followed by approximately 600 million more before that person "breathes his last" or "fights to his last breath." In the interim, he will spend some time "waiting with bated breath." He will hold his breath in anticipation, and enjoy "breathtaking" scenery. He will feel "out of breath" on occasion, and "take a breather" to recover. When comfortable and out of danger, he can "breathe freely." When nervous, he's told to "take a deep breath and settle down."

Through this lifetime of respiration, he will sometimes feel "inspired"—a word that also means to take in air. He may work closely with others and "conspire"—breathe together. It goes on until he "expires"—breathes out for the last time.

Although the importance of breathing is reflected in our vocabulary and in common lore, few people pay attention to breathing; it just seems to happen. But breath control is a key component of emotional control and hence performance control, for each of the Internal Energy States has a typical breathing pattern.

BREATHING PATTERNS AND INTERNAL ENERGY STATES

High Intensity

HIGH POSITIVE	HIGH NEGATIVE
Energy without tension	*Tension with energy*
Deep, regular abdominal breaths, frequency tied to performance.	Shallow, irregular rapid thoracic breaths, not tied to performance.

Pleasant _____ **Unpleasant**

LOW POSITIVE	LOW NEGATIVE
Neither energy nor tension	*Tension without energy*
Less frequent breaths, quite regular and deep.	Shallow, regular thoracic breaths.

Low Intensity

The Internal Energy State can determine the breathing pattern, but it works both ways. The breathing pattern can control the Internal Energy State.

TRY IT AND SEE

When we first performed this experiment at one of our workshops, we were skeptical. All we asked people to do was pant—breathe rapidly, shallowly, and irregularly. After two minutes of panting, we asked several people how they felt. Without exception, they said they were worried, almost panicked; they felt threatened. They were in the same safe, quiet room they had been in five minutes earlier; no outside threats had entered to alarm them. The change in their emotional state arrived solely because they had changed their breathing patterns.

Try it yourself. Start breathing quickly, taking shallow, irregular breaths. Close your eyes; you'll find disquieting imagery. When this was done in laboratories, the psychologists found all the symptoms of incipient panic—elevated blood pressure, faster heartbeat, a rise in epinephrine and norepinephrine levels, a loss of blood flow to the peripheral regions and digestive tract, and more blood going to the large muscles.[3]

A few minutes of panting can trigger the stress response out of a clear blue sky; other breathing exercises can put you in control.

AIRBORNE STRATEGIES

At breath clinics, we have taught upward of two dozen breathing techniques; every one of them works for certain situations. The most important breath techniques, however, are those that will move you into the desired Internal Energy States.

In the High Negative, one typically feels tense and threatened; the major need is to calm down, relax, and move over onto the Positive side. How many times have you told someone to "take a deep breath and calm down"? Or had someone tell you that?

The Deep Abdominal Breath

The best way to take that deep breath and calm down is with the Deep Abdominal Breath. You can do it at any time while sitting or standing, but it's easiest to learn while lying down in a private, quiet place.

1. Lie on your back with your hands on your stomach— between the bottom of your rib cage and your navel.
2. Push your stomach out; feel your hands rise.
3. After your hands start to rise, allow yourself to inhale through your nose. For a count of one–two, "aim" the breath at your abdomen; follow that with a three–four count, "aiming" the breath into the lungs.
4. Now, exhale. Breathe out of your chest for a one–two count, then out of your abdomen for a three–four– five–six–seven–eight count.
5. Push your stomach out and start the process again.

Practice this for a few minutes each day; once you're familiar with the sensations, you'll have no trouble doing it while standing up. Whenever you feel tense—whenever you find yourself holding your breath or breathing rapidly and shallowly—take a few Deep Abdominal Breaths to move you over into the Low Positive.

The Contrived Yawn

The Low Negative is the state of boredom, marked by shallow, regular breaths. It's a signal that you should be going to sleep; at the least, you're not much interested in the visible world. When you force yourself to stay awake in this state—it seldom does much for your career if you're seen snoozing at your desk or nodding off when the supervisor is talking—your body responds with a yawn: a deep breath to enliven the nervous system with some oxygen.

To get out of the Low Negative, though, you don't have to wait for a natural yawn. Start one of your own. Stand up, raise your hands high overhead, push out your navel, and take in all the air you can. Exhale vigorously, and repeat this three or four times. You'll shift from Low Negative to Low Positive.

Moving from Low Positive to High Positive often occurs automatically; when a challenge presents itself, you adjust your breathing without conscious effort. But there will be

times when you want to control the switch, and there are
two breathing techniques that work well for this.

The Ha! Breath

This can be done while sitting, walking, or running;
ideally it is done while standing.

1. Tilt your head back and inhale deeply through your
   nose.
2. Exhale forcefully through your mouth, issuing a loud
   "Ha!" sound that originates in your lower abdomen.
3. Repeat as needed.

In places where it is inappropriate to bark, you can issue
a quieter sound, or just a forceful breath.

This breath comes automatically with a good laugh—
another reason why humor so often accompanies top-flight
performance. Athletes often use a variant of it—the grunts
of tennis players as their rackets meet the ball, or of weight
lifters as they hoist the iron.

The Ha! Breath provides an instant infusion of oxygen
into the bloodstream, thus providing more fuel for the
brain and body—which means instant energy for top-flight
performance.

The Energy Breath

This works well when you feel relatively happy, but sluggish; it moves you from the Low Positive to the High
Positive.

1. Stand, with arms at your sides, relaxed but in good
   posture.
2. On a slow, steady inhalation, raise your arms outward
   until they reach shoulder level. Then move your arms
   in front of you, and raise them over your head.
3. Hold your breath for a moment.

4. Exhale out of your mouth as if you were blowing a candle. As you exhale, drop your head, shoulders, and neck.
5. Repeat five to ten times.

The Relaxing Breath

It is every bit as important to be able to move from High Positive to Low Positive as it is to move from Low Positive to High Positive. Controlling energy is the key to outstanding performance, mental or physical. Great performers don't waste energy by staying in the High Positive when the situation calls for a relaxed, Low Positive state.

To shift by breath control is about as simple as counting past three. Inhale slowly through your nose, silently counting one–two–three–four. Hold the breath for two counts. Exhale slowly and deliberately, counting one–two–three–four.

You'll be in good form, and when the next challenge comes at you, you can meet it with a Ha! Breath or an Energy Breath.

ADVANCED TECHNIQUES

For many athletes, it is vital that they learn to coordinate their breathing with their performance—perhaps best exemplified by the grunting and whooshing of tennis players and weight lifters. It is just as important in less vigorous sports that demand fine motor coordination; archers and sharpshooters learn to time their relaxed breathing with the release of the arrow or their pull on the trigger.

But the demands of other careers are much more complex and much less sudden; the ball that's coming at you isn't always visible, nor is the target you aim toward. If your work is analogous to those sports, you can apply some of their breathing techniques. Most work isn't; you use breathing to control the Internal Energy State, and good

performance results from a High Positive Internal Energy
State.

There are, however, a couple of more specialized
breathing techniques you might try in certain common
workday situations.

The Patience Breath

1. Do a slow Deep Abdominal Breath with a long, relaxed
   exhalation. (If the line you're stuck in is a traffic jam,
   however, don't breathe too deeply. Suffice it to say that
   carbon monoxide is something you don't want to un-
   necessarily expose your brain cells to.)
2. As you exhale, think of something relaxing. Try to visualize it as clearly as possible.

Alternate Nostril Breathing

The theory behind this technique lies in the two hemispheres of the brain behind the two nostrils of the nose.
Through the breathing day, people favor one nostril or
the other. The left nostril will dominate for a while, taking
in most of the air; after ninety to one hundred minutes,
this will switch to the right nostril.

The right brain hemisphere controls the left side of the
body; the right hemisphere is the center of creative, image-
oriented, non-verbal processing. The left hemisphere,
verbal and logical, controls the right side. If there's a connection between hemispheres and nostrils, it would be that
the left nostril stimulates the right hemisphere, and vice
versa.[4]

A team of researchers at the Salk Institute for Biological
Studies, headed by David Shannahof-Khalsa, attached
electroencephalographs (EEGs) to the heads of volunteers.
The researchers found that one cerebral hemisphere always showed more activity than the other. However, the

activity alternated between hemispheres every ninety to one hundred minutes. Since the timing resembled that of the nostril dominance cycle, they compared the two.[5]

When the left nostril was dominant, the right brain hemisphere—the image side—was most active. When the right nostril dominated, so did the left hemisphere—the linear side.

Alternate Nostril Breathing stimulates both hemispheres; it works this way:

1. Do a few relaxing Deep Abdominal Breaths.
2. Close your right nostril with your right thumb and inhale through your left nostril for four counts.
3. Close your left nostril with your right ring finger (both nostrils are closed) and hold your breath to a count of eight.
4. Open your right nostril and exhale through it for a count of eight.
5. Inhale through your open right nostril for a count of four.
6. Close your right nostril and hold your breath for a count of eight.
7. Open your left nostril and exhale for a count of eight.
8. Repeat the sequence for five to ten minutes.

It's not simple, and it leads to unfamiliar sensations— mental imagery amid bodily calmness. But it's worth a try.

This suggests another technique. If you're stuck for an idea or an image, hold your right nostril shut, and inhale and exhale only through the left nostril for five to ten minutes. The studies at the Salk Institute show that this increases electrical activity in the right half of the brain, stimulating creativity. Conversely, if you've got a head full of ideas but the situation calls for close focus and analysis, hold your left nostril shut for a few minutes. You should find yourself in a logical, analytic mode, ready to tackle a spreadsheet or edit a proposal.

AS YOU LIVE AND BREATHE

The power of breathing mystifies most people, even many who have mastered the techniques. But it isn't so mysterious once you look at how air goes through the body to touch the mind.

Outside air generally starts its journey to the brain in the nostrils, wherein grow small hairs that catch any of the larger troublemakers—everything from dust to insects—that may be about in the atmosphere. Just behind the nose are three bony projections, called the turbinates.

Lined with a moist mucous membrane and covered with millions of tiny hairs, the turbinates form chambers for the air to circulate through before it goes any farther. A trip through the turbinates further filters the air, because the tiny hairs and sticky mucous surfaces trap the particles that got past the nostril hairs. The air is also conditioned in the turbinates—it picks up body heat there, thus allowing the lungs to function at a constant temperature without being chilled by inrushing cold air. If the air is dry, it will become more humid by passing over the mucous membrane.[6]

After the air has been sampled, cleaned, warmed, and humidified by the nostrils and turbinates, it passes into the windpipe, a rather prosaic piece of biological plumbing, three-fourths of an inch in diameter, that leads to the lungs.

High in the windpipe operates a valve, the epiglottis, that allows air to come in from the mouth as well as the nose. This has survival value—air is so important that the body needs an alternative intake if the nose is blocked. Further, the mouth can gulp in air more quickly than the nose; the mouth is so much bigger that it requires only half as much energy to draw in air that way. When the body is demanding a lot of oxygen in a hurry, it usually comes in through the mouth.

The mouth, however, lacks an extensive filtration system. And because the air moves so quickly, it isn't warmed or conditioned properly. Cold, dry air goes straight to the lungs. The air takes up moisture from the lungs, impairing their efficiency. The cold air absorbs heat from the lungs; cross-country skiers have frostbitten their lungs when they started gulping from the subzero atmosphere.

Breathing through the mouth saves energy in only one respect: It takes less effort to pull air through the mouth than through the nostrils. But in every other way, it is less efficient than breathing through the nose. It's something for emergencies; it shouldn't be a habit.[7]

However the air comes in, it descends through the windpipe, which splits into two smaller tubes, one for each lung. This splitting continues inside the lungs, ending in tiny tubes called the bronchioles. At the end of each bronchiole are tiny air sacs, not unlike miniature balloons, called the alveoli. They handle the major function of breathing—getting oxygen into the bloodstream.

The walls of the alveoli are lined with blood vessels whose walls are only one cell thick—about one fifty-thousandth of an inch. When you breathe in, oxygen passes through the wall and is picked up by the hemoglobin in the red blood cells. In the same breath, the cells release the carbon dioxide that they have picked up elsewhere in the body; the carbon dioxide goes the other way through the wall, accumulates in the lungs, and goes out when the lungs exhale.[8]

PUMPING AIR

Of its own accord, air won't move from the external world into the innermost recesses of the body with sufficient speed to prevent asphyxiation. It must be forced in and out.

In this respect, the lungs function much like a set of bellows—like those on an accordion. To bring air into the bellows, the musician stretches the accordion. This creates more internal space and drops the air pressure inside, causing a partial vacuum. Air rushes in through the openings to equalize the pressure. When the musician squeezes the bellows, it raises the pressure inside, forcing the air out.

Three sets of muscles can expand the lungs, so that air will enter. Lean back for a minute, and you can try all three.

First try touching your ears with your shoulders. Unless you're a contortionist, your shoulders didn't get there, but you inhaled sharply when you tried. Lifting the shoulders expands the chest cavity, reducing air pressure in the lungs. To equalize the pressure, you inhaled.

Now try thrusting your chest out. Again, you expanded the volume of your chest cavity, and air came in. The scientific term for the chest cavity is the thorax; this kind of breathing is known as thoracic breathing.

Finally, push your navel out. This doesn't visibly expand the chest cavity, but the air comes in—and it's a deeper breath this time as well. Why?

Below the lungs is a wall of muscle that separates the lungs from the rest of the interior of the torso. The diaphragm—that wall of muscle—can move up and down. When it goes down, as it does when you push your navel out, it expands the chest cavity. Air rushes in. When it comes up, it reduces the volume, pushing the air out.

When you use the diaphragm, it takes about 1 percent of the body's ongoing energy consumption to bring air in and out. Thoracic breathing is only about half as efficient; it takes twice as much muscle energy to accomplish the same work.[9] No studies have surfaced on "shoulder breathing" ("clavicular respiration" sounds more scientific), but you can easily conduct your own: Try it for a few minutes and see how tiring it is. Breathing with the diaphragm uses less energy, freeing more for whatever else you want to be doing.

GETTING IN DEEP

Another benefit to breathing with the diaphragm (also called deep breathing or belly breathing) is that it takes air deeper into the lungs than thoracic breathing does. Thoracic breathing brings air only into the top parts of the lungs; fresh air reaches the lower regions only by diffusion, and waste gas accumulates.

You spend most of your waking hours sitting or standing. Blood is forced through the lungs by the heart, but it is still subject to gravity's pull. The blood tends to accumulate in the lower parts of the lungs. Typically, the blood is flowing at 0.07 liters per minute—that's about a tablespoon—at the top of the lungs. In the middle, it's better than a pint a minute, and at the bottom, the flow is more than a quart per minute.[10]

Yet with thoracic breathing, almost all the fresh air is in the upper parts of the lungs. The essence of breathing is to bring blood and oxygen together; thoracic breathing concentrates each in a different part of the lungs.

Deep breathing with the diaphragm comes naturally; watch a sleeping baby. Her belly will rise; as it rises, she inhales deeply. If it comes that naturally—babies start breathing that way all on their own—and it's so much more efficient, then why do most people avoid deep breathing and spend their days with short and shallow thoracic breaths?

That's difficult to answer; we honestly don't know. Perhaps social convention—a puffed-out chest, on woman or man, is considered manifestly more attractive than an expanding and contracting belly. Or maybe American clothing styles, which tend to fit tightly around the waist, just make it too uncomfortable to breathe sensibly.

AUTOMATIC PILOT

Breathing normally takes place without conscious effort; it is regulated by several complex mechanisms in the central nervous system that are still not fully understood.

Normal breathing—the way you breathe when you aren't thinking about how you're breathing—appears to be controlled primarily by specialized nerve cells at the base of the brain and the top of the spinal cord. This area is the core of the brain's limbic system, which generates emotions and controls the flow of messages from the brain to other parts of the body. Thus breathing is quite closely tied to emotional state; they're controlled by the same part of the brain.

The nerve cells that regulate breathing—the respiratory control neurons—are sensitive to fluctuations in blood chemistry. When the carbon dioxide exceeds a certain level, these cells send a message that it's time to inhale. They control the frequency of breathing and the depth of each breath. The more carbon dioxide there is in the blood, the more oxygen is needed and the deeper is the breath.

Yawning, a familiar reaction to boredom or drowsiness, is simply the body's way of trying to get more oxygen. When not much is going on, or you're not much interested in what's going on, your brain and body require little oxygen. Breathing consequently becomes shallow. Repeated shallow breathing sets up a pattern in the respiratory control neurons; the pattern there influences the nearby reticular formation in the brain. The reticular formation controls whether you're awake or asleep; a continuous shallow breathing pattern brings on sleep. To stay awake, the body must force in more oxygen. Thus the yawn—a big, deep breath.[11]

The respiratory control neurons can also be triggered from other parts of the brain, which is why you can, to some extent, control your breathing. You can hold your breath if you have to pass through a room filled with toxic gas, or if you're swimming. If sufficiently strong-willed, you can hold your breath until you lose consciousness; then the automatic system will take over.

Because breathing is both voluntary (that is, subject to conscious control) and involuntary (an unthinking product of body chemistry and emotional state), it provides a way to use voluntary thought to control involuntary processes. The breath of life links the voluntary and involuntary parts of your nervous system.

BREATH AND EMOTION

The relationship between breath and emotion is easy to observe. People breathe easily when relaxed and calm; they pant when agitated. Boredom produces a shallow breathing pattern that leads to yawns in an effort to stay awake. Holding your breath —try it for thirty seconds—reduces the flow of oxygen to the brain; nervous sensations are thus not perceived as intensely as when breathing is regular. For that reason, people in pain tend to hold their breath as they grit their teeth. Tension causes irregular breathing—you hold your breath in anticipation. The typical stress reaction—the fight or flight response—dynamically alters breathing.

When the alarm goes off, it's because the organism perceives a threat. The muscles around the chest contract, making breathing more difficult. There's a reason for that; the tense muscles make it that much harder for an enemy's spear or a saber-toothed tiger's claw to penetrate the wall around the body's vital organs.

Since deep breathing is impossible within a constricted chest, breathing becomes more rapid and shallow as the body attempts to get enough oxygen. The body also shifts its metabolism so that less oxygen is needed; the muscle cells resort to lactose fermentation for energy, instead of combining glucose with oxygen. Carbon dioxide, the waste product of normal glucose–oxygen metabolism, can be carried off in the blood and excreted through the lungs. But lactose fermentation gives off lactic acid, which just builds up and causes pain in the muscles. The only way the lactic acid can be hauled off is to combine it with oxygen. So the body builds up an oxygen debt that must be satisfied with continued deep breathing, once the emergency is over.

Breathing patterns may be tied to personality traits. Dr. Sheila Sperber Haas, a psychologist at New York University, studied 160 healthy adults in 1979 and 1980. She found differences in breathing patterns that could not be explained by differences in body build or oxygen demands.[12]

Slow, deep breathers, she found, were "strong, stable and adventurous, intellectually and physically in control of their lives." The rapid, shallow breathers, she discovered, were "shy, passive, fearful and dependent on others for a sense of self and security."

It leads to one of those chicken-and-egg questions. Did members of one group breathe slowly and deeply because they were "strong, stable and adventurous"? Or were they "strong, stable and adventurous" because they breathed deeply? Other research points out that the signals in human nerves go both ways; emotions control breathing, and breathing can control emotions. Each is a function of the other. Since performance levels are determined by emotional state, it means that breath control leads to greater performance control.

This was known ages ago. One of the oldest known medical texts is the *Nei Ching*, written about 2600 B.C. in China. One passage points out that "the lungs are the ministers who regulate one's actions." Aristotle, writing two millennia later, said, "The soul is air . . . Air that we breathe gives us the soul, life, and consciousness." Pantanjali, who codified yoga 1,800 years ago, stressed that the control of breath was the key to controlling emotions, thoughts, and performance.[13]

WHAT BREATHING WON'T CONTROL

Breathing, no matter how well controlled, is not the answer to every challenge. Breath control won't make one lose weight, and it won't make one stop smoking.

Deep breathing stimulates, rather than deadens, the appetite. However, many people who have weight problems are compulsive eaters; they're nervous, so they chomp down a doughnut or some potato chips. Deep breathing relaxes, thus reducing the compulsion to grab some food. Also, slow, rhythmic breathing during meals means slower eating. That gives the body time to digest the food, and to signal the brain that it's no longer time to send out hunger signals.

As for smoking, it's a question of motivation. Breathing won't provide the motivation. The more that smokers learn of the wonders of the respiratory system, however, the more motivation they may gain to quit. They may come to agree with King James I of England, who nearly four centuries ago said of smoking: "Herein is not only a great vanity, but a great contempt of God's good gifts, that the sweetness of man's breath, being a good gift of God, should be willfully corrupted by this stinking smoke."[14]

The gift of breath is the gift of life; the control of breath means the control of life, and control is what top performance is all about.

9
HUMOR:
The Power of Mirth

IDEAL PERFORMANCE STATE: MOOD CONTROL

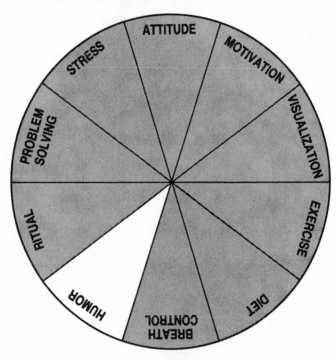

STRATEGIES

Humor creates a playframe for problem-solving.

Humor reduces defensiveness and improves communication, while neutralizing stress.

Use humor to get into the High Positive.

In 1964 Norman Cousins, the author of more than a dozen books and then editor of *Saturday Review*, felt his body start to fall apart. His physicians had a name for the problem—ankylosing spondylitis—and an explanation: The collagen, the tissue that connects tissue to bone, was coming unstuck. Cousins found it difficult to move his arms and legs, or even to roll over in bed; at one point, his jaws almost locked.

His regular physician offered about one chance in five hundred of recovery from this little-known disease; the specialist said he'd never seen a recovery. About all the two could predict with confidence was that if the affliction didn't kill Norman Cousins, he'd never stand or walk again.

Cousins left the hospital and checked into a hotel. He foreswore the usual medications for a regimen of mirth: Marx Brothers movies, Thurber essays, Three Stooges shorts, E.B. and Katharine White's *Subtreasury of American Humor*, and some "Candid Camera" episodes (generally those featuring embarrassed doctors and nurses) sent over by his friend, Allen Funt.

As a painkiller and analgesic, laughter worked at least as well as phenylbutazone, colchicine, and codeine. "I made the joyful discovery," Cousins wrote, "that ten minutes of genuine belly laughter had an anesthetic effect and would give me at least two hours of pain-free sleep."[1]

His connective tissues began to regenerate. Using humor, Cousins regained his health and continues as a top performer: He has written additional books, traveled extensively to lecture and consult, surmounted a major heart attack, and joined the medical school faculty at the University of California in Los Angeles.

Cousins launched something of a medical revolution. "I've been gratified that many hospitals across the country have incorporated humor as a standard part of their treatment," he told us. "In any illness, one of the intensifying factors is panic, and the panic is a disease in itself. If you get people laughing, that serves as a blocker for panic. It's sort of a bullet-proof vest."[2]

HUMOR AND INTERNAL ENERGY STATES

Like the other strategies for controlling your emotional state, humor enables you to move almost effortlessly from

CHARACTERISTIC HUMOR OF INTERNAL ENERGY STATES

High Intensity

HIGH POSITIVE *Energy without tension*	HIGH NEGATIVE *Tension with energy*
Characteristic Humor:	Characteristic Humor:
Pervasive spirit of fun Creating jokes Joking with companions Detached perspective Quiet smiles	Aggressive humor Ridicule Sarcasm Satire Sardonic laughter

Pleasant _____|_____ **Unpleasant**

LOW POSITIVE *Neither energy nor tension*	LOW NEGATIVE *Tension without energy*
Characteristic Humor:	Characteristic Humor:
Relaxed and receptive; laugh at others' jokes Laughter ranges from chuckles and giggles to guffaws	Gallows humor Sick jokes Effort to laugh Laughter seldom loud, few smiles

Low Intensity

one Internal Energy State to another in most cases. Each state has a characteristic kind of humor; moving from state to state can be as simple and pleasant as finding a new source of mirth.

LOW NEGATIVE HUMOR

When something strikes you as "funny" in this state, you frown before you laugh, and you usually don't laugh at all. When you do, it's generally a feeble imitation. People in the Low Negative seldom create, or respond much to, any humor.

What little humor does emerge is "gallows humor"—an effort by the powerless to make the intolerable bearable. A good example is the joke often heard when a company is contracting in the face of economic problems and employees are being laid off: "What's the difference between this company and the *Titanic*? The *Titanic* had a band."

But you are not powerless, and that is why you should avoid this kind of humor. You may be bored, morose, disgusted, light-years away from being a top performer, but the mirthless pathos of gallows humor merely perpetuates this state.

When you're in the Low Negative, you do hear or see things that really are funny. You start to laugh, hard and loud; you change Internal Energy States instantly. Where you arrive depends on the type of humor you responded to.

THE HIGH NEGATIVE WEAPON

High Negative humor is cynicism, sarcasm, and ridicule. The High Negative, after all, is the aggressive "fight or flight" zone, and its humor is not the mirth of joy, but a potent form of aggression and hostility. It is unpredictable —you can't control where the storm will hit.

How potent is this kind of humor? At the turn of the century, Collis P. Huntington owned the Southern Pacific Railroad and controlled California politics. Huntington had similar influence in Washington, where Congress was considering a law that would allow the Southern Pacific to postpone repaying hundreds of millions of dollars the railroad owed the government. Huntington understandably wanted the bill to pass and went to Washington to lobby personally. Most newspapers of the era opposed the "Refunding Bill," but they presumed it would pass. Huntington was one of the richest and most powerful men in America; no one had the bank account or the political clout to defeat him.

But Huntington had run afoul of William Randolph Hearst, the newspaper baron who liked a good fight. Hearst didn't fight Huntington with money, nor did he print scathing exposés about corruption and the Southern Pacific. Hearst instead used an even more powerful weapon: High Negative humor. He hired Ambrose Bierce, the "Bitter Bierce" who wrote *The Devil's Dictionary*, to go to Washington and comment upon Huntington's lobbying there.

Bierce peppered his articles with biting humor. Of a Huntington appearance before Congress, Bierce wrote: "Mr. Huntington appeared before the committee and took his hands out of all pockets long enough to be sworn." Similarly entertaining accounts continued for several months, and jokes about Huntington circulated from coast to coast and among the Washington elite. Despite his power and money, it quickly became impossible to side with Huntington. Even congressmen whom Huntington had bribed voted against the Refunding Bill; they were too embarrassed to support him.[3]

High Negative ridicule, carefully applied, brought down Collis P. Huntington when money and raw political muscle had no effect; such is its power. And some powerful people know the uses of ridicule and sarcasm. "Humor? It's great," explained David Mahoney, former CEO of Norton Simon Inc., an international consumer marketing company. "I use it a lot, though sometimes I have found that what I think is amusing offends somebody."[4] Mahoney was among those featured in a 1980 article in *Fortune*: "The Ten Toughest Bosses." But the subordinates' comments about those ten were revealing—the men at the top often employed ridicule and humiliation, cruel blasts of High Negative energy, to enhance their power.

But they loosed the tornado as well.

High Negative humor, when deployed inside a company, is a deathblow to morale: All ten companies were noted for high turnover rates among their executives. Good people won't tolerate it for any longer than they have to. Those who stay find themselves in the Low Negative, employing black gallows humor to make their careers tolerable. Here's what a subordinate said of Robert Stone, CEO of Columbia Pictures: "[He's a] galley master who, hearing that the rowers would die if the beat were raised to 40, would say, 'Make it 45.' "[5] The creative impulse that went into that bit of Low Negative humor might have made a fine script for the studio under different circumstances— but whoever said it found that cynicism was the only way to make life there tolerable.

Using humor negatively leads to two problems. It's aggressive, so people fight back—they get into a negatively charged state as well, and deploy their own weaponry of ridicule. This epidemic of nastiness saps productivity, since energies are being directed into creating more barbs. And as invective is slung, more people get hit. Those who can't compete slide deep into the Low Negative, the state of depressed performance, while throughout the affected areas, trust breaks down.

In our corporate workshops, we've found the hardest situations to repair are those resulting from High Negative humor. Nobody trusts anybody, and everyone is afraid. The recipients are afraid of ridicule, and the jokesmith is sure that everyone will try to get even with him when his back is turned. To be honest, we haven't found an easy way to bring teamwork back to such a group. Typically, we explain why it happened and help people understand what happens to self-confidence and teamwork when someone continually ridicules those he works with.

It is interesting to note that High Negative humor appears to have no tie to performance; the companies whose "tough" CEOs deployed it did not outdistance those whose CEOs did not ridicule and humiliate others. Unless you're manufacturing satire, High Negative humor does nothing to improve business performance; in fact, our research shows that it produces the poorest of work environments. It's merely a way to summon a thunderstorm, with no guarantees that the tornado will strike its intended target. Tornadoes are powerful enough—the average twister has enough energy to light a small city for a year—but it's all destructive power.

When you're in the Low Negative, and something makes you laugh, it can put you in the High Negative if it's High Negative humor. But there isn't any consistent way to use humor to get out of the High Negative. The more you create, the crueler your jokes become. Sometimes a dose of other humor, something from the Positive side, will make you laugh uproariously, relax you, and take you to the Positive side. The most consistent route out of High Negative humor, we have found, is exercise. Work off that aggression, instead of telling someone, "You want a new career that suits your talents? Go find a village that doesn't have an idiot." Exercise will lead to relaxation; you'll slide over to the Positive side.

If you're the target of High Negative humor, you're at the receiving end of what Mark Twain called the most powerful weapon in the human arsenal. But responding in kind will put you in the same negative state, a place to avoid. Black humor and withdrawal, the most common reactions, push you into the Low Negative. The ideal response is to move to the Positive side, perhaps through breath control or visualization; High Positive humor, with its paradoxical involvement and detachment, gives you the mental toughness to overcome even the awesome powers of High Negative humor.

LOW POSITIVE FUN

When you're in the Low Positive, you don't create many jokes—but you respond to the humor of others. Relaxed and receptive, you're recharging your batteries.

Just how revitalizing this state can be was demonstrated by Norman Cousins when he checked in at the Marx Brothers Clinic; his body healed more quickly with mirth than it could have with any other known medicine.

Low Positive humor is a reliable way to relax; one of the most curious but effective techniques is the "laugh tape," which is just that. The ten-minute track of titters, guffaws, giggles, and mirthful howls is so ludicrous that when we've put it on at a workshop, it has never failed to put everyone in stitches—even a very staid and straitlaced assortment of accountants.

However they bring it on, top performers find that laughter is not only extremely relaxing, but the only sedative that allows one to stay alert. You can't be tense while you're indulging in a belly laugh—for instance, you can grip something tightly when you're angry or in a dozen other emotional states, but about all you can hold when you're laughing is your sides. Muscle tension vanishes during laughter.

Scholars of humor, from Aristotle to Freud, explain that almost all humor is built on a redirected anticipation.[6] You are led to expect one thing—and then comes the punch line, which redirects that anticipation. The building mental tension is reflected in nervous and muscular tenseness, and the punch-line laughter provides a release. That may explain why kings kept jesters at hand; it also explains why situation comedies are so popular on television during the early evening hours, when people want to unwind after a day's work.

What's wonderful about this relaxation of tension is that a laugh generally releases more than its share. It springs not only the tension that was built up during the joke, but also any other tenseness lurking in your system, and it does so in mere seconds.

In the Low Positive, the body and mind are relaxed, yet attentive; for one thing, you're watching or listening for the next joke.

When you want people to listen to what you're saying, you want them to be relaxed and attentive—in the Low Positive. Making people laugh is the most certain way to put them into the Low Positive; this is why virtually all successful politicians, lecturers, and salespeople start a presentation with a joke and are masters at interjecting them appropriately as the presentation proceeds.

Continued hearty laughter can become an energizing force, because it forces deep breathing with the diaphragm. More oxygen reaches more blood, and so more energy reaches the brain. Dr. Perry Buffington calls laughter "internal jogging," thanks to this effect.[7] Starting the day with a few minutes of laughter isn't just pleasant: It's a tool for building mental energy. And a "laugh break"—something that many top performers build into their schedules without quite realizing precisely why—removes accumulated tension while refilling the energy reservoir.

The power of humor to enhance attention while it refreshes and stimulates has not been ignored by some productive organizations. Jim Henson's Muppets, in short videotapes, now star in meetings from Citibank to the Central Intelligence Agency; it was IBM that sought out the Muppets almost two decades ago, and some two thousand companies have followed suit. They've found that humor pays. People pay more attention, and leave meetings with a positive attitude, when the meeting includes a few minutes of Kermit the Frog and his corporate cronies, among them Leo, the vice-president of dubious affairs, who's always coming with a PLAN (Packaged Line Analysis Nexus) that's BAD (Bold And Decisive) and BIG (Business Improvement Guaranteed).[8]

One major insurance company went a step further. Instead of using humor to leaven its meetings, it sent its middle managers to meetings that were nothing but humor: laugh-therapy sessions. Productivity went up 44 percent in three months as a result of reduced tension and increased energy.[9]

PERFORMANCE HUMOR

When you're using the energy without feeling any tension, you're in the High Positive. Hearty laughter can carry you into the High Positive; the laughter disappears as the performance ensues. But the feelings that led to the laughter will remain, for the High Positive has its own form of internal humor.

A High Positive performance occurs in a state of fun. The sense of joy that accompanies every great performance can even be accompanied by mirthful laughter.

Getting to the performance, however, requires preparation and practice and a lot of hours that don't provoke much in the way of laughter.

Writers love to write; most of them find the requisite research a boring chore. Good managers enjoy making decisions, but filing and reading reports and going to meetings are usually about as exciting as watching grass grow. Mechanics like to troubleshoot and fix machines, but they find it hard to work up much enthusiasm for routine maintenance and cleaning and putting the tools away. Athletes get fired up for the game, but find themselves lagging at practice and dreading it.

Every arena where anyone performs has its routine and scutwork. These can't be sloughed or ignored; they must be done and done well. No matter how banal, boring, routine, trivial, or mundane they may seem, they require good performance.

The prospect of going to the library for six hours to dig up one useable anecdote generally won't push a writer into the High Positive. But if she isn't in that aware, probing state, she may well miss the obscure incident she's looking for. Her solution is to get into the High Positive by using humor first. Once she's there, she can turn to her research with commitment, confidence, and control. It isn't scut-work any more.

Such humor insures stamina, the persistence required for accomplishment. Renn Zaphiropolous, co-founder and president of Versatec, is reputed to be the funniest man in Silicon Valley. He defines business as providing a service for a profit. "If you provide the service and make no profit, that's philanthropy," he explained. "If you make a profit and provide no service, it's thievery." His sense of humor, he said, "has given me the courage to go through some rough times."[10]

Lee Iacocca credits a sense of humor for the stamina he displayed in pulling Chrysler through the lean years at the start of the decade. Even at its worst, in 1981 when the debt was mounting and the Michigan State Fairgrounds were overflowing with unsold cars, he could still laugh when someone asked him about his one-dollar-a-year salary: "Oh, don't worry. I spend it very carefully."[11]

This humor, used by top performers to keep themselves on track, sometimes makes no sense to an outsider. Or it seems brutal and insensitive, as is the case with the emergency room humor that surgeons sometimes display. Patients aren't supposed to hear it (on "M*A*S*H," however, the audience did, and it was the most popular show in America for most of a decade). Surgeons in an emergency room cannot afford to be tense; the laughter, based on what's before them, keeps them loose but focused. We patients may not appreciate the humor, but we do appreciate the results.

CREATIONS

High Positive humor is the creative state; you look for humor so that you can sustain it and it can sustain you. One way to define humor is to look at it as the intersection of two thought systems, and this, also, is the font of creativity.

Consider an old joke for illustration:
"Sir, may I have your daughter's hand?"
"Why not? You've already had the rest of her."
In the first line, the word *hand* is used in a figurative sense from the courtly and romantic tradition of chivalry. In the reply, *hand* is literal—one part of a body that has other parts, too—with an interpretation from another system of thought. The two intersect, and there's a joke.

Looking for humor in the High Positive means looking for those intersections. It also represents the ability to psychologically distance yourself from problems so that you are not entangled by them. The sense of humor puts you into what Max Eastman called "the state of fun"—the Ideal Performance State, where you enjoy the problems.[12] Humor is another form of creative thinking—finding new uses for old items, imagining new processes and products, devising innovative approaches. The process is the same; the mind is in the same state. As William James pointed out, genius "means little more than the result of perceiving in an unhabitual way."[13] The habitual way, most of the time, is sequential; humor, like creativity, is lateral, a jump to the side, or even off the table.

Humor means shifting the frame of reference. Dr. Nathan Kline revolutionized the treatment of mental illness with his introduction of modern tranquilizers in 1953 and 1954 at the start of his brilliant, discovery-packed career. Seldom were those discoveries what he originally sought, but Kline employed humor to find ways to use what he found. The tranquilizer chlorpromazine had been used to treat victims of tuberculosis; he was called in because the drug wasn't working. The treatment reduced depression, but the victims felt so good that they over-exerted themselves and their tuberculosis got worse, negating any benefits from the drug.[14]

A logical solution might have involved imprisoning the patients or adding sedatives to the medication. But Kline exploited the irony and saw it in a different light. Chlorpromazine may not have done much for tuberculosis, but it sure fought depression.

Kline, thanks to his sense of humor, was able to see this irony and exploit it. Forget about using chlorpromazine to treat tuberculosis, he said. Use it to fight depression instead, since it's so good at that. The result was a revolution in the treatment of mental illness. "The great changes in science," he explained, "have been . . . the result of a shifted frame of reference" accessed by humor. "You have to be a little whimsical."

Recent neural research points out that humor starts in the right hemisphere of the brain. When something strikes you as funny, that's where you realize it; the electrodes show activity there that leads to laughter. When you make up a joke, the new relationship is realized on the right side and the concept goes to the left side where it is verbalized. The right side finds the relationships; the left side analyzes. From what is now known of the process of creativity in the mind, it is identical to humor—perception on the right side, expression and analysis on the left.[15]

Having a "sense of humor about things" leads to the detachment that is part of the High Positive. Laughing at yourself—finding humor in your own actions—is a way of stepping outside yourself and your limits. It allows you to perform in the seemingly paradoxical state of being involved and detached at the same time. Time and time again, we've heard those words when we've asked people to tell us how they felt during their best performances.

A sense of humor is often a reliable indicator of top performers in all fields. Very few jobs, for instance, are anything like a job interview. Most jobs, especially high-level positions, involve vision, applied psychology, diplomacy, and the ability to inspire and motivate people. So how does an interviewer judge executive talent during a simple talk?

William Gold, a headhunter and executive vice-president of the Association of Executive Search Consultants, is one of America's foremost executive recruiters. A sense of humor, in his view, probably outranks an MBA and a fast-track résumé. He would never offer a job, he says, to some

humorless hopeful. "What companies are seeking is someone who can see issues clearly. If a person can laugh, particularly at himself, he can probably step back and get the
right perspective on things."[16]

Being able to find humor in any situation means more
than just finding the proper perspective. It means that you
have a powerful tool that you can use to control your response. The key to mental toughness is focusing on what
you can control. With the tool of humor, you can learn to
choose a response that keeps you on the positive side.

COMMUNICATION

Dr. Harvey Mindess, a scholar of mirth, calls humor the
shortest distance between two people.[17] As we have pointed
out, humor generally makes people relaxed and attentive,
thus improving communication. That's just a start.

Good-spirited humor—poking fun at oneself—also es-
tablishes rapport and builds teamwork. Say what you will
about Ronald Reagan's politics, he's a master at communicating with the public with self-deprecating humor. After
the assassination attempt in 1981, he looked up in the
hospital room and saw himself surrounded by doctors and
nurses. "If I had received this much attention in Holly-
wood," he told them, "I never would have left."[18] Thanks
to his sense of humor, people can dislike his policies, but
they don't get mad at him—so he can still exercise leadership. Few presidents in recent history have had Reagan's
sense of humor, and their leadership suffered as a result.

Just as laughter alleviates tense muscles, it eases tense
situations. When Eugene Cafiero was president of Chrysler, he faced a troubled plant in England full of militant
employees. Upon his arrival, a burly union man announced, "I'm Eddie McClusky and I'm a Communist."
Instead of worrying about an international conspiracy in-
vading one of his plants, Cafiero extended his hand and
said, "How do you do? I'm Eugene Cafiero, and I'm a

Presbyterian." The tension was diffused by the ensuing laughter; the plant kept running.[19]

Humor is just as important at home; a participant in one of our workshops explained a tense situation involving himself, his wife, and his son. His son had altered grades on his report card; mother was understandably angry at the attempted deception. No son of hers was going to cheat. The son said she was putting on too much pressure for good grades. Communication stopped there. When the father—our workshop participant—walked in, she told him to handle it. Upon examining the report card, he announced that his son was a terrible student: "You couldn't even pass forgery." Everyone laughed—and then they talked about it.

BETTER THAN THE GRAPEVINE

The enhanced two-way communication is a valuable tool for anyone who has to deal with other people, but merely listening to the jokes around you can provide information you could get nowhere else. Humor betrays grievance: It's a socially acceptable way for people to express their dissatisfactions. If someone finds your diction annoying, for instance, he might not call that to your attention—but he may well start telling jokes that mimic your accent. If you're an employer and you start hearing your employees comment about how they stuck two of your paychecks into a gumball machine and nothing came out, you might well examine your wage scales. Humor is a lateral approach that avoids confrontation while still conveying the message. As George Bernard Shaw pointed out, "If you're going to tell people the truth, you'd better make them laugh. Otherwise they'll kill you."[20]

Using humor in communication provides instant and honest feedback. You know right away if you're getting across—if they don't laugh, then either they're not listening or you're not communicating. And you know if you're being understood. "Yes men" can fake appreciation for a marketing plan and comment on its insight and precision while they actually think the opposite, but Ed McMahon is probably the only person in America who can convincingly fake a laugh.

DEVELOPMENT AND EXERCISE

"Men will confess to treason, murder, arson, false teeth, or a wig. How many of them will own up to a lack of humor?" said Frank Colby. He has a point. At every workshop, we ask several questions about this and related topics. We ask people if they personally know anyone who does not have a sense of humor. A few hands generally go up —further investigation shows that the participants are referring to creditors, employers, and occasionally, their spouses. Judging by that response, we'd have to grant that there must be some people who do not have a sense of humor.

Then we ask them to raise their hands if they believe they have a sense of humor. Every hand goes up—except from one person, who's trying to be funny. Our conclusion —and that of psychologists who've studied the subject— is that everyone has a sense of humor. If it's not doing all that it can for you, then you need to develop it.

Laughing more is a good way, although there are some social problems with this. If you're a banker who sits in one of those glassed-in offices visible from the lobby, people might believe that you were not taking your responsibilities properly if they saw you during a laugh break. Until public attitudes change—a few years ago, remember, it was imprudent for a banker to be seen jogging on a public thoroughfare—you'll have to close the curtains or find someplace else to take your break.

Further, you might be tempted to laugh at inappropriate times. It isn't like stifling a sneeze, wherein the impulse dissipates with time. If you don't laugh, the tension will accumulate and you'll get more nervous and edgy. So as soon as possible—as quickly as you can get out of the courtroom or away from the self-important customer with the glowing purple tie or the foreman who thinks you're goofing off on company time if you're smiling—laugh. If you have to induce it, induce it. Put on the laugh tape or pull out a copy of *The Sotweed Factor* or *Truly Tasteless Jokes*.

If your performance requires creativity—and these days, whose doesn't?—then start making it a habit to see the mirth in everything that comes before you. Think of five or ten perfectly ridiculous uses for everything on your desk, workbench, or lab table. One of them might be practical, and even if that doesn't happen, you'll be paying much closer attention to your tools and procedures than you were paying—an effortless step into the High Positive.

You may be in charge of something—an office or shop or production line or whatever. Make it an environment where laughter is welcome and cherished. Encourage people to post cartoons and quips on the bulletin board. If you see people freeze in mid-laugh when you walk in unexpectedly—tell a good one, so that they'll release their tension and get back to a productive happy environment.

You are always in charge of yourself; build humor into your life wherever you can. Not all the medical results are in yet, but we can assure you of one thing: Developing your sense of humor won't hurt you.

WHY IT WON'T

The precise cranial wiring and plumbing of mirth is not yet as well understood as the processes of stress and tension. It's easy to get people to feel tense when they're wired up to EKGs and galvanic skin resistance monitors and technicians are taking blood samples. But it's really difficult to get people to laugh under the same circumstances; the psychobiology of humor remains largely unexplored.

But scientists have come up with some explanations.

They started by calling laughter "the luxury reflex."

Laughter is a reflex—an unthinking response to a stimulus, like a knee-jerk after a tap under the patella, or the pupil of the eye constricting in bright light. Laughter is a "luxury" because it isn't necessary for survival in any traditional sense; every other animal (the hyena doesn't laugh; its bark sounds like laughter) seems to manage well enough without laughter.[21]

Laughter, however, is not a luxury, but nature's own remedy to the "fight or flight" state if it gets turned on needlessly.

Something alerts you; that perks up the electrical flow in the reticular activating center at the core of the brain. The limbic system, which controls your emotions, gets the stimulus, and sends out small amounts of norepinephrine: Pupils dilate, pulse and respiration speed up, etc. You're ready to act.

But most often these days, the action you were ready to take—to club some tiger senseless, for example—is inappropriate. You can take it out on something else. You can withdraw so that nothing more will alert you. You can let it build so that you're even more edgy, nervous, tense, and harried. Or you can laugh.

As nearly as anyone can figure, humans developed laughter before they developed speech; otherwise, given the tensions that exist in any social group, our ancestors probably would have slain each other before they figured out how to hunt mammoths together.

AN OLD CONNECTION

Humor, top performance, and health are intimately related, although Norman Cousins's demonstration of their tight relationship came as something of a surprise to the medical community a decade ago. Humor has yet to show up in the standard pharmacopoeia with the antibiotics and tropane alkaloids, but some hospitals have added "mirth wings," and the usually staid *Journal of the American Medical Association* in 1984 published an article about the energizing and healing effects of humor.[22]

The connection between humor and health extends to the roots of Western medicine. Hippocrates and Galen believed that four fluids—blood, phlegm, bile, and black bile—circulated within the body. Health and happiness resulted from the proper balance of these fluids; the Latin word for fluid is *humor*.[23]

When one humor was produced to excess, the result was disease or disturbance. Too much phlegm, and the victim was "phlegmatic": sluggish and unexcitable. An overload of bile (the Greeks called it *chole*) made one "bilious" or "choleric": short-tempered and irritable. Black bile to excess had its own word: melancholy. If blood (the Latin word was *sanguis*) was in surplus, the victim was "sanguine": optimistic and unaccountably cheerful. To cure this, doctors bled the patient; such bleeding was George Washington's last medical treatment.

During Washington's lifetime, the word *humor* came to be applied to the traits of those people who were ostentatious about exhibiting a surplus of one humor or another. The sight of an over-humored soul—bilious or sanguine or melancholic or phlegmatic—made people laugh. Thus humor came to mean something funny, and its connection to performance and health was lost when surgeons ceased to practice in barber shops.

Since then, however, medical researchers have discovered dozens of bodily chemicals called neurohumors—acetylcholine, epinephrine, dopamine, serotonin, and the endorphins—that circulate in minuscule amounts through the brain and bloodstream to control emotional states, and thus health and performance. High-level performance, in a way that Galen and Hippocrates never suspected, is indeed the product of a balance of humors.

The stimulus that starts laughter releases norepinephrine—the neurohumor of alertness, which leads to edginess and aggression if too much is released. Many suspect, although the evidence is not conclusive, that this output of norepinephrine stimulates the production of endorphins, the body's answer to opium; this would account for laughter's ability to reduce or eliminate pain.

It is fairly certain that with laughter, the limbic system releases serotonin, whose full effects are little studied. But when its levels rise high enough in the brain, ecstasy and euphoria result, and this may account for the undiluted pleasure of a good laugh. Serotonin also helps return the bodily processes back to normal from the alert stage— digestion resumes, pulse and respiration slow, etc. Yet alertness is not impaired; somehow the mind and body receive the benefits of both the sympathetic and parasympathetic portions of the autonomic nervous system, giving you energy without tension.[24]

A good dose of laughter brings those humors into the proper balance. Norman Cousins demonstrated how laughter can heal an "incurable" disease; our own work and play have convinced us that humor is a tool for mental toughness. Humor provides relaxation, focus, creativity, control, and perhaps most importantly, Positive Internal Energy.

Whether it's time to illuminate a vast expanse with a peak performance, or to relax and recharge your batteries, laughter is no laughing matter. As Lord Houghton said, "The sense of humor is the just balance of all the faculties of man, the best security against the pride of knowledge and the conceits of the imagination, the strongest inducement to submit with a wise and pious patience to the vicissitudes of human existence."

10

PERFORMANCE RITUAL:
Finding the Ultimate Groove

IDEAL PERFORMANCE STATE: MOOD CONTROL

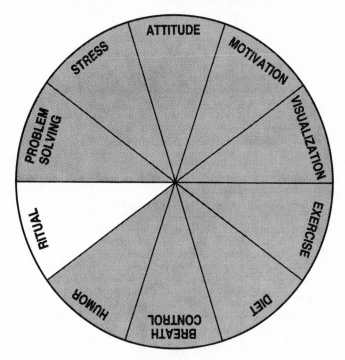

STRATEGIES

The surest way to employ and enjoy the strategies of mental toughness is to build the strategies into rituals and habits.

Everyone goes through a ritual to prepare for a performance, although many rituals actually militate against good performance.

Develop rituals that work for you, not against you.

Outside the operating room, the surgeon scrubs, going through a routine he established early in his residency. Its steps are so familiar to him, from bending over the sink to placing his trained hands inside the latex gloves, that he is barely conscious of the procedure; his mind is focused on the upcoming challenge. Before entering the operating room, he tenses, crosses himself, and then strides toward the anesthetized patient, ready to begin his performance.

The attorney has been over and over her material; it's the summation and she dare not come in unprepared. Her courtroom performance today will determine several futures. Ten minutes before the bailiff calls the court to order, she opens the folder and glances through it once again. In place is the 18-carat gold Cross pen that came with her promotion to full partner. After a glance at it, she closes her eyes and envisions herself, confident and forceful, making her case.

Major league hitters wiggle and stretch, wave their bats, and shuffle their spikes until they are set for the first pitch. A well-known hockey player tries to wear the same shirt to every game; when the shirt got left behind once on a road trip, his playing suffered. An actress insists on eating the same meal precisely ninety minutes before the curtain rises each night. An executive always lights a cigarette before taking a telephone call—even when he already has one going—though he seldom smokes on other occasions. An entrepreneur swears that his ideas will dry up if he does not spend forty minutes of each working day immersed in hot water, starting at 7:15 A.M.

Performers use rituals to prepare for performances.

THE ROLE OF RITUAL

You have already developed certain rituals that you go through to prepare for your performances. They probably started in elementary school, the first time you had to stand up and talk to the class, and you have been adding to your pre-performance routine ever since. The rituals assure you that it is time for a performance, that you are ready to perform, and that you can perform. Your pre-performance rituals move you from one Internal Energy State to another.

Ideally, rituals relax tension while building energy, so that you can be in the High Positive when you perform. Some pre-performance rituals, however, work against you. If the rituals become superstitions, then you're asking for trouble.

What's the difference between a ritual and a superstition?

A ritual is the routine you follow to prepare for performance at your best; the best rituals rely on factors within your control and insure that you are indeed ready for the performance. Superstitions depend on something beyond your control, and are negative. You know that you'll do better if you follow your ritual, but you're scared that something terrible will happen if you don't abide by a superstition.

Finding Your Rituals

When we explain pre-performance rituals at our workshops, most people catch on immediately. Others, however, tell us that they have no such rituals—they are not slaves to superstition or habit.

If you cannot think of any rituals that you go through before performing, ask the people you work with and the people you live with. You may not have noticed just how you ready yourself for a performance, but those around you have. You'll learn surprising things about yourself: You always check your hem or fly (even when you're sure) before rising to greet anyone, or you always rummage through your top desk drawer (never, of course, coming up with anything that you might use) before you settle

INTERNAL ENERGY STATES RESULTING
FROM COMMON PRE-PERFORMANCE RITUALS

High Intensity

HIGH POSITIVE	HIGH NEGATIVE
Energy without tension	*Tension with energy*
Can result from:	Can result from:
Calming rituals (exercises and breathing patterns that reduce muscular and nervous tension)	Chemical stimulants (caffeine, nicotine, amphetamines, cocaine)
Energizing rituals (exercise and breathing, as well as visualization into the performer's role)	Rituals which build energy without reducing tension (tensing when the telephone rings or someone comes in; visualization that involves negative or vengeful imagery)
Rituals tied to the specific performance—they assure you that all is ready; the routine enables you to focus on the performance instead of worrying whether everything is in order.	Rituals tied to a different performance; you are angry because you aren't prepared for this performance.

Pleasant ——————————————————————— **Unpleasant**

LOW POSITIVE	LOW NEGATIVE
Neither energy nor tension	*Tension without energy*
Can result from:	Can result from:
Relaxation rituals (breath, exercise, visualization, and humor)	Superstition (you've knocked on wood or stroked the rabbit's foot, but you're worried that you haven't done enough)
Alcohol or other depressants	
Comforting rituals (religious, social)	Abuse of alcohol or other depressants

Low Intensity

down to work on a new project, or you cannot answer a question without leaning back in your chair and then rocking forward.

Good rituals, damaging rituals, and superstitions are all ways to prepare for your performance by adjusting your emotional balance. For better or worse, they represent an effort, usually unthinking, toward the relaxed energy of the Ideal Performance State.

Let's look at various response routines to a common performance situation.

Instant Performance

As soon as your secretary announces the call, you wish you were on assignment in Arabia. It's someone who has a right to be perturbed, who wants some good answers, who isn't going to settle for any excuses. You don't even have plausible excuses, let alone good answers.

Superstition: You'd prefer to believe otherwise, but you cannot help believing that this happened because you forgot to arrange your desktop pens this morning before you checked your appointment calendar. Maybe knocking on wood will help, so after a couple of taps on the desk veneer, you feel up to picking up the phone.

This superstition probably started because on one day that things went really well, you set up your pens before checking your calendar. As a ritual, it is as good a way as any other to make sure everything is in place before you start to perform; it is like the batter's routine before he gets set for the first pitch, or the surgeon's before an operation.

There's nothing intrinsically wrong with knocking on wood (or any other insensate object) in order to release tension.

But these have become superstitions because they allow you to avoid responsibility for your own performance. If the call resolves the problems, then you'll have difficulty believing that you performed well—you'll credit the wood.[1] There are many ways to build your confidence, but this is definitely not one of them. If the call doesn't go well, then you can blame those unruly pens, or perhaps the morning horoscope. That's easier than examining your performance and noting where it could be improved.

Damaging Ritual: Light a cigarette, have a drink, or reach for a snack.

We don't need to belabor the well-known health hazards of smoking here, nor do we need to explain how nicotine is one of the most addictive drugs known to science. A great number of cigarettes, however, are not lit in response to that urgent chemical demand from an addicted physiology wherein every cell seems to be screaming for a fix, but instead as part of a misleading visualization ritual.

Examine the people in cigarette ads—they're calm yet energized, vibrant and interested, full of life. In short, the models are portraying the High Positive. Many smokers form the image of themselves at their best as something that happens because they lit a cigarette, thanks to the fortunes that the tobacco companies spend to promote these images.

Even if smoking did nothing to damage health, it would generally impair performance. The drug nicotine is a central nervous system stimulant—a cigarette actually increases nervous tension while decreasing physical energy. Despite the ads and their imagery, reaching for a cigarette pushes the smoker away from the High Positive and toward the High Negative. It works against good performance.[2]

If you smoke, many of the cigarettes you light every day are an effort to prepare for a performance rather than a response to the addictive demands of nicotine. Realizing this means that you can change your imagery of you performing at your best. That's not going to make you quit, but it will help, and that's a start.

Alcohol and tranquilizers also militate against performance. They indeed relax, but they diminish intensity. At best, these depressants lead to the Low Positive, which is not a performance state. Within reason, alcohol eases tension while enhancing social situations. At worst, alcohol and sedatives are physically damaging and addictive pathways to the Negative side.

Some people, feeling anxious and tense, will reach for a snack—a ritual that can impair immediate performance and adversely affect long-term health and energy.

Smoking, drinking, snacking—they're all established and esteemed in common lore as ways to prepare yourself to handle a stressful situation. It can be difficult to free yourself from thirty or forty years of such practices. Just remember that common responses to challenges lead to the common outcome—losing and suffering from stress-related disease.

Good Ritual: Quickly prepare for performance with two enhanced shrugs, three abdominal breaths, and a visualization.

When you heard who was calling, you felt the tension and anxiety build. The enhanced shrugs relax you, and the deep breaths build energy. Even so, some anxiety might come through in your voice, if you focus on controlling your voice—so you visualize yourself at your best as you pick up the telephone.

The pair of shrugs, three deep breaths, and a momentary image constitute the ritual you have developed for situations that call for prompt and intelligent responses. It moves you from the Low Positive into the High Positive, where you perform at your consistent best. You've experimented, especially with the imagery, to develop this ritual, and you'll continue to experiment. It's so interesting and involving that you almost look forward to those challenging calls.

This was the first High Positive performance ritual you developed. Now you're developing a ritual to prepare yourself for those times when you need to solve problems or be creative. So far, the ritual that has worked best in preparing for extended performances (those marathon quality-control seminars) has been visualization, but there are some exercises that you'd like to try.

BUILDING RITUALS

The first step in building your performance rituals is to know when—in what situations—you now rely on rituals (good, bad, or superstitious). If you always reach for a snack or knock on wood in a given situation, then that situation represents a potential source of stress—a challenge. Monitor your Internal Energy States closely to see whether your ritual is working for you or against you.

Then experiment with the strategies of emotional control—especially humor, breath control, exercise, and visualization—until you develop the short sequence of strategies which will move you into the High Positive so that you are at your best when you meet the challenge.

It is vital that you monitor your Internal Energy State before and after your experimental rituals. The monitoring represents immediate feedback, which is essential to learning anything well. Most deaf people, for instance, have no physical impairments to their tongues, lips, and vocal cords which would prevent them from speaking well. Because they cannot hear, though, they get no feedback, and never develop the precise and complex mind-body coordination required for speech.

At first, your strategic responses will not be rituals. You'll have to stop and think and make yourself go through them. Even small rituals take time and discipline to evolve from mental checklists into habit and instinct. You didn't develop your current rituals overnight, and you won't change them that quickly, either. The brain holds your ritualistic responses strongly and deeply; these responses might best be understood as channels through which the impulses always tend to flow in given situations. Developing new performance rituals means establishing new patterns of neural connections that will become "channels" with practice and repetition.[3]

How long it takes to establish a new ritual depends on many factors, the major one being how frequently you can practice and then use the ritual. Something you do twenty times a day will be established that much more quickly than something you do once a week.

This may sound like a long and difficult process, but most likely you have already mastered a similar, and perhaps more demanding, challenge. Remember when you learned to drive? If you were like most teenagers, you had awesome positive motivation—it was what you wanted to do more than anything else in the world. But your first hours behind the wheel were spent in white-knuckled desperation. With uncoordinated feet, you pressed the brake and gas pedals at the same time. The gearshift, if the car had one, seemed enough of a mystery when the car was parked, let alone while moving. Every twist of the steering wheel pointed the car toward a place you didn't want to go.

Many of your intuitive responses were totally inappropriate, as you discovered on a slick street when you jammed the brake pedal, instead of pumping it, and you tried to steer away from, instead of into, the ensuing skid.

Within a month, though, control of the gas pedal, brake, clutch, gearshift, and steering arc were established as rituals—the right responses were becoming graceful and automatic, instead of the hesitant result of a pained and hurried perusal of your memory. In weeks, you had come most of the way toward mastering more than a ton of powerful, complex, confusing, and potentially lethal machinery.

NIGHT BY NIGHT

Developing the strategies of emotional control into ingrained responses will improve your performance dramatically as your rituals begin to work for you, instead of against you.

Sustained excellence, however, demands tremendous quantities of energy. If the energy isn't there to operate your mind and body at capacity, then your performance will suffer. Developing that energy means building emotional control strategies into your daily routine.

We've already explained the importance of diet and exercise; another major factor is sleep. A healthy adult generally requires from six to ten hours nightly. The total function of sleep remains something of a mystery to science, but the evidence suggests that sleep is more important to your brain than to your body. When volunteer research subjects are deprived of adequate sleep, they maintain their physical strength; what suffers are mental skills like perception, abstraction, and reasoning.

While you sleep, your brain sorts through the day's events. Most recent memories are examined and then ignored, while others are assigned to short-term and long-term memory. This classification process is generally known as dreaming.[4]

In our work with executives, entrepreneurs, and athletes, we often hear, "I can get by on four or five hours of sleep a night. That's all I need."

Invariably, it isn't all they need. There's an easy way to find out how much sleep you need. Unplug your alarm clock. You'll wake up when you've had enough sleep, and not before—and you'll discover that you actually need more sleep than you've been getting. Your overall performance will improve, although you will have to adjust: Retire earlier, of course, and make sure that you start moving right away in the morning. One good tactic is ten or fifteen minutes of aerobic exercise as soon as you awake.

Changing your sleep routine, as well as establishing a performance diet and an exercise schedule that builds mental stamina, is not something that you can or should do all at once and overnight. Focus on one aspect at a time—diet is one of the best places to start—and build it into your life. Once it is firmly in place, develop another long-term strategy.

CHARTING YOUR COURSE

The principles of mental toughness are simple and direct. Implementing those principles requires persistence, dedication, and monitoring.

To monitor your progress toward full implementation of these strategies, we recommend that you make copies of the following chart and fill it out completely for three weeks—twenty-one days. Plan on about twenty minutes each evening. We've included a sample.

This close monitoring of your routines and rituals is not a mere exercise. You are conducting a vital experiment, and you are both the experimenter and the subject. You are determining the relationships between your pre-performance rituals and the quality of your performances, and you are establishing the pattern of mental toughness strategies that best works to keep you performing at your best.

This is exactly the same method we use with executives, entrepreneurs, and athletes when we work with them personally. No mentor or coach can stay at your side and advise you how to be at your best for each performance; it's a skill that you must develop on your own. The strategies are tools, and the monitoring shows you how these tools affect your performance every day. A challenging world lies before you.

DAILY PERFORMANCE MONITOR

Date _____

ENERGY MANAGEMENT
Internal Energy State

1 hour after rising _____   Late morning _____

Early afternoon _____   Late afternoon _____

Evening _____   Comments _____

Challenges and Potentially Stressful Situations

1. Event _____

_____   Initial Energy State _____

Mental Toughness Strategy _____

Energy State during Performance _____   Comments _____

_____

2. Event _____

_____   Initial Energy State _____

Mental Toughness Strategy _____

Energy State during Performance _____   Comments _____

_____

3. Event _____

_____   Initial Energy State _____

Mental Toughness Strategy _____

Energy State during Performance _____   Comments _____

_____

4. Event _____

_____   Initial Energy State _____

Mental Toughness Strategy _____

Energy State during Performance _____   Comments _____

_____

5. Event _____

_____   Initial Energy State _____

Mental Toughness Strategy _____

Energy State during Performance _____ Comments _____

_____

6. Event _____
_____ Initial Energy State _____
Mental Toughness Strategy _____
Energy State during Performance _____ Comments _____

_____

7. Event _____
_____ Initial Energy State _____
Mental Toughness Strategy _____
Energy State during Performance _____ Comments _____

_____

8. Event _____
_____ Initial Energy State _____
Mental Toughness Strategy _____
Energy State during Performance _____ Comments _____

_____

FOOD, MOOD, AND SLEEP

Hours slept on preceding night _____

Mood at waking _____

Meals and Snacks

Time _____ Contents _____

_____

Time _____ Contents _____

_____

Time _____ Contents _____

_____

Time _____ Contents _____

_____

Time _____ Contents _____

_____

Time _____ Contents _____

_____

Time _____ Contents _____

_____

Overall

Red Meat _____ Sweets _____

Drugs

Caffeine _____ Nicotine _____ Alcohol _____

Other _____

Comments _____

_____

EXERCISE

Aerobic Type _____ Duration _____
Exercise Type _____ Duration _____

Other   Type _____ Duration _____

         Type _____ Duration _____

VISUALIZATION AND IMAGERY

Description _____

Result _____

Description _____

Result _____

Description _____

Result _____

BREATH CONTROL

Occasion _____

Breathing Method _____ Result _____

Occasion _____

Breathing Method _____ Result _____

Occasion _____

Breathing Method _____ Result _____

Occasion _____

Breathing Method _____ Result _____

Occasion _____

Breathing Method _____ Result _____

HUMOR AND RELAXATION

Positive Humor	Negative Humor
Number of mirthful jokes told or created _____	Number of malicious or 'gallows' jokes told or created _____
Number of good laughs at mirthful humor _____	Number of occasions that it caused laughter _____

Comments _____

_____

_____

Relaxed times

Occasion _____   Comment _____

Occasion _____   Comment _____

Occasion _____   Comment _____

Occasion _____   Comment _____

Occasion _____   Comment _____

Grade the day, A through F, for the following

Creativity and problem solving _____   Feeling in control _____

Positive attitude _____   Time Management _____   Motivation _____

Confidence ___ Energy Management ___ Negative Energy Control ___

Meeting of personal goals _____ Meeting career goals _____

Overall performance _____ Comments _____

Strategies to try in the future _____

_____

SAMPLE DAILY PERFORMANCE MONITOR

Date ___Oct. 15, 1985___

ENERGY MANAGEMENT
Internal Energy State

1 hour after rising ___Low Neg___   Late morning ___Low Pos___

Early afternoon ___Low Pos___   Late afternoon ___High Pos___

Evening ___Low Pos___   Comments ___Slow, bad start today, picked up.___

Challenges and Potentially Stressful Situations

1. Event _Phone rang at 6:30. Only a wrong number but it annoyed me_
and I couldn't get back to sleep **Initial Energy State** ___Low Neg___

Mental Toughness Strategy ___Energizer breaths—I finally got up.___

Energy State during Performance _N/A_ **Comments** ___Felt groggy___
for my first hour or two.

2. Event ___Boss upstairs didn't like my latest report. Said I'd have___
to improve. _____ **Initial Energy State** ___High Neg___

Mental Toughness Strategy ___Tension-reducing exercises___

Energy State during Performance _High Pos_ **Comments** _Didn't back_
down. Asked for specifics and got some clear answers I can implement.

3. Event _Lunch with important client who always makes me feel nervous._
_____ **Initial Energy State** ___High Neg___

Mental Toughness Strategy ___Visualization (rehearsal) and breath___

Energy State during Performance _High Pos_ **Comments** _Didn't make_
the sale I wanted to make, but they're still interested.

4. Event _Outline our section's contribution to the new marketing plan._
_____ **Initial Energy State** ___Low Pos___

Mental Toughness Strategy ___10 minutes of quick exercise—the stairs___

Energy State during Performance _High Pos_ **Comments** _Started on a_
negative note, but once we were going, we did well. It's good work.

5. Event _Some jerk cut me off on the freeway and I missed my_
usual exit. _____ **Initial Energy State** _High Neg (kill!)_

Mental Toughness Strategy ___Deep relaxing breaths___

Energy State during Performance <u>Low Pos</u> Comments <u>Found a new</u>
<u>way home that might be shorter and faster.</u>

6. Event _____

_____ Initial Energy State _____

Mental Toughness Strategy _____

Energy State during Performance _____ Comments _____

_____

7. Event _____

_____ Initial Energy State _____

Mental Toughness Strategy _____

Energy State during Performance _____ Comments _____

_____

8. Event _____

_____ Initial Energy State _____

Mental Toughness Strategy _____

Energy State during Performance _____ Comments _____

_____

FOOD, MOOD, AND SLEEP

Hours slept on preceding night _____ 6 1/2 _____

Mood at waking _____ Rotten _____

Meals and Snacks

Time __7:15__ Contents _Toast, jelly, coffee_____

_____

Time _10:30__ Contents _Apple, chunk of cheddar_____

_____

Time _12:30__ Contents _Steak sandwich, fries, salad, coffee—_
made me groggy for a while after I got back

Time __3:15__ Contents _An orange and some crackers_____

_____

Time __7:00__ Contents _Chicken, baked potato, steamed_____
asparagus, tossed salad, 2 drinks

Time __10:15__ Contents __Glass of milk and some chocolate cake__

Time _____ Contents _____

Overall

Red Meat __4–5 oz. in steak__ Sweets __Jelly, cake__

Drugs

Caffeine __4 cups cof.__ Nicotine _____ Alcohol __2 drinks__

Other __2 aspirin—morning headache, probably from not enough sleep__

Comments __Got to watch those late snacks and big lunches—I should__
find a new restaurant to take clients to.

EXERCISE

Aerobic Type __stairs__ Duration __10 minutes__

Exercise Type __daily 3-mi run__ Duration __25 minutes__

Other Type __tension-reducing__ Duration __30 sec to 1 min__

Type _____ Duration _____

VISUALIZATION AND IMAGERY

Description __Mental rehearsal of client lunch__

Result __Was prepared for everything that happened__

Description __Tropical island fantasy__

Result __Fell happily to sleep last night__

Description _____

Result _____

BREATH CONTROL

Occasion __Getting woken up by wrong number__

Breathing Method __Energizer__ Result __Got going__

Occasion __Relax tension before and during client lunch__

Breathing Method __Abdominal__ Result __No jitters__

Occasion __Weaving moron on freeway__

Breathing Method __Deep and calm__ Result __Quit being angry__

Occasion _____Resting before sleep last night_____

Breathing Method ____Regular and shallow___ Result ____Nodded off___

Occasion _____

Breathing Method _____ Result _____

HUMOR AND RELAXATION

Positive Humor	Negative Humor
Number of mirthful jokes told or created ___2___	Number of malicious or 'gallows' jokes told or created ___3___
Number of good laughs at mirthful humor ___8___	Number of occasions that it caused laughter ___6___

Comments The negative came when we were making fun of the competition after lunch, starting the marketing plan. It switched to positive once we got going.

Relaxed times

Occasion ___after run___   Comment _always_____

Occasion ___after dinner___ Comment _watched a comedy on tv_

Occasion ___in bed___   Comment _____sex relaxes, too___

Occasion _____   Comment _____

Occasion _____   Comment _____

Grade the day, A through F, for the following

Creativity and problem solving ___A___ Feeling in control ___B___

Positive attitude ___C___ Time Management ___C___ Motivation ___B___

Confidence _A_ Energy Management _B_ Negative Energy Control _B_

Meeting of personal goals ___C___ Meeting career goals ___B___

Overall performance ___B___ Comments Need to address the problems they found in my reports.

Strategies to try in the future _Try some exercise during lunch hour_ and avoid those big meals; should make my afternoons better.

11

PROBLEM-SOLVING AND CREATIVITY:
Breakdown is Breakthrough

IDEAL PERFORMANCE STATE: MOOD CONTROL

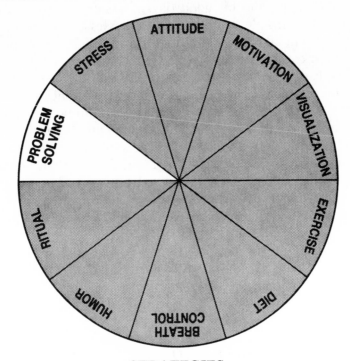

STRATEGIES

Creativity and problem-solving are the same process.

Your most creative times come when you are in the Ideal Performance State.

Use the strategies of mental toughness to increase creativity as well as to sustain the energy required to turn ideas into reality.

"Every man who writes, or paints, or composes knows by hard experience that there are days when his ideas flow freely and clearly and days when they are dammed up damnably. On his good days, for some reason quite incomprehensible to him, all the processes and operations of his mind take on an amazing ease and slickness. Almost without conscious effort he solves technical problems that have badgered him for weeks. He is full of novel expedients, extraordinary efficiencies, strange cunnings. He has a feeling that he has suddenly and unaccountably broken through a wall, dispersed a fog, got himself out of the dark. So he does a double or triple stint of the best work that he is capable of—maybe of better work than he has ever been capable of before—and goes to bed impatient for the morrow. And on the morrow he discovers to his consternation that he has become almost idiotic, and quite incapable of any work at all."[1]

Nearly seventy years have passed since H. L. Mencken wrote "The Divine Afflatus" and pondered the abiding mystery of creativity and problem-solving: Why do the ideas flow so freely on one day, indeed during one hour, and dry up on the next?

By posing the question in his exuberant and humorous style, Mencken provided the key to its answer. His description of the creative state sounds familiar because it is identical to accounts of the Ideal Performance State—"almost without conscious effort," "amazing ease," "far better work." The writer coining phrases, the sales representative anticipating the clients' questions, the engineer perfecting an elegant process, the financier devising junk bonds and poison pills—they all perform in the same emotional state. The only difference is the nature of the performance.

A BESMIRCHED REPUTATION

Performance and productivity are justly esteemed, but creativity could use a better reputation. Creativity is often presumed to be the exclusive quality of poets starving in garrets, artists on the verge of a nervous breakdown occasioned by drug addiction, inventors seeking venture capital for perpetual-motion machines, and advertising copywriters just this side of sanity. Most people are prudent, reliable, and trustworthy, and the others are creative.

Nonsense.

Creativity comes as standard equipment with every fully configured human nervous system, and every child delights in being creative—in finding new ways to look at the world and new ways to do things. Studies of children indicate that creativity is strong in all children up to about age ten. Then it declines in most people because they perform in an environment that values certain different qualities—sitting still, listening to directions, abiding by the accepted ways of doing things—more highly than creativity.[2]

No matter how long they lie idle, however, the creative abilities remain, dormant but ready, like seeds that can bloom only in the proper environment. Insofar as it is possible to test for creativity, the results show that creativity is present in all people with normal or higher intelligence. Further, there is no correlation between creativity and other forms of intelligence (or whatever it is that they measure on I.Q. tests). Some creative people are highly intelligent, some aren't, just as some highly intelligent people score in the lower ranges for creativity. What is significant is that the quality is present in everyone.[3]

Much of the American business environment is pervaded by a deceptive illusion that creativity may be fine in its place—and that place is the campus or the artists' colony, not the Real World, which runs on profits and productivity. However, profit comes from goods and services which necessarily result from insight, innovation, and invention: creativity. Without creativity, corporations stagnate, decline, and disappear. Creativity—the ability to identify and solve problems—makes the Real World go round.

CREATIVE STATES

The emotional constellation of the creative state and the emotional constellation of the Ideal Performance State are identical. As we pointed out at the beginning of this book, the Ideal Performance State depends on so many variables that there is no consistent, repeatable way to attain it. The strategies of mental toughness give you the ability to control your emotional state so that you consistently perform in the High Positive. Since the High Positive is the gateway to the Ideal Performance State, performing in the High Positive means that you will spend much more time in the Ideal Performance State.

Does this mean that creativity only comes to you fortuitously?

To some extent, yes, because you are at your creative best in the Ideal Performance State. Creativity, however, is like other mental skills: It can be developed and enhanced. You'll be better at it at some times than at others, but you can always be very good. And the strategies of emotional control can be applied to improve your ability to identify and solve problems.

WHERE IDEAS COME FROM

When we put on a workshop open to anyone who wants to register (as opposed to a workshop for a single company), we find that the only thing the participants generally hold in common is a desire to perform more consistently at the upper range of their abilities. To the abstract expressionist painters and the new wave poets, better performance means more creative drive, and the same is true, although to a lesser extent, for the commercial artists, technical writers, engineers, marketing managers, product developers, and software writers. "Creative accounting" is not a flattering term in that profession, but accountants are fully aware that their best performances come when they can see patterns among the numbers and come up with good advice for their clients.

When discussing creativity, we go around the group and ask the participants how they felt and what they were doing when they got their best ideas. We're never surprised by their descriptions of how they felt when the ideas were flowing—calm yet energized, relaxed but confident, immersed in what they were doing. They were in the High Positive.

What was surprising, at first, was that the ideas that arrived during those creative times often bore no relationship to what the person was doing. An advertising campaign which had produced much frustration and no clear concept materialized in shining clarity during a hard-fought racquetball game. An elegant assembly-language subroutine sprouted while the programmer cut parallel turns on a black-diamond ski run.

Why was it that, when these performers moved into the High Positive while skiing or playing racquetball, they had creative insights that had nothing to do with the slope or the court? Why was it that Henri Poincaré made one of his greatest mathematical discoveries while on a geological expedition?[4] What is it about the High Positive that brings forth unrelated insights and solutions?

A LEFT AND A RIGHT

The answer seems to lie in the two hemispheres of the frontal part of the brain—the "right brain" and "left brain" that have provoked so much talk over the past decade. The discovery that the two hemispheres process information

differently led to a Nobel Prize in 1981 for Dr. Roger
Sperry of the California Institute of Technology.[5]

The discovery also led to an epidemic of pseudoscience
and pop psychology, as millions of Americans were told
that they had spent their lives enslaved by the evil linear
left hemisphere, and that their potential would be actual-
ized if they would just learn how to tap into the wondrous
holistic right hemisphere. It wasn't quite that simple. Glowing promises remain unfulfilled, replaced by an understandable suspicion of right-brain miracles.

The frontal hemispheres handle most of your conscious
acts—speech, writing, adding, drawing, throwing, catching, etc. They divide the work of controlling the body, with
each hemisphere responsible for the opposite half of the
body. When you move your left arm, it is a consequence
of neural activity in the right hemisphere, and vice versa.

Each hemisphere perceives and processes information
differently. At birth, the hemispheres are separate but equal;
if one is damaged in infancy, the other hemisphere can
take over all its functions and the child will grow up with
normal abilities. But by age five, the two hemispheres are
no longer mirror images.

The "dominant" hemisphere is generally the left, which
makes sense. It controls the right side of the body, and
most people are right-handed. The left hemisphere tends
to process information sequentially; it specializes in words
and numbers, in analysis and convergent thinking; it controls speech.

You can illustrate this specialization fairly easily if you
need to convince yourself. (And if you're right-handed.
There are two ways of being left-handed, one of which
this will apply to, if you reverse the directions; the dis-
tinction is too complex to go into here.) Hold out your
right index finger and balance a pencil on it sideways. Then
try to talk.

You'll find it quite difficult to converse while keeping
the pencil balanced because the left hemisphere is trying
to do two things at once—to handle the precise coordi-

nation of breath and delicate muscles required for speech and the delicate adjustments necessary to keep the pencil from falling off your finger. Balance the pencil on your left index finger, and you won't have any trouble keeping it there while you talk—the right hemisphere is taking care of that while the left carries on the conversation.

The right hemisphere tends to process information as patterns, rather than sequences; as images, rather than arbitrary symbols; as synthesis and divergence rather than analysis and convergence. Although the right hemisphere is not mute, it does not handle verbal information well; its vocabulary appears limited to short and simple words. When you confine your thinking to words, the right hemisphere has difficulty transmitting its perceptions and insights.

A problem that has been troubling you might well be identified and solved on the right side. On the left, all the techniques to verify and implement the solution can be at combat alert. But unless the two halves are working together, the problem remains a problem.

When the two halves work together, poets find their rhythms, athletes get into the groove, and accountants know how to improve cash flow. It requires a right and a left, and getting into the High Positive brings both up to speed.

That's why creative insights and long-sought solutions so often materialize during unrelated but pleasant and energizing activities. The writer has the concept on the right side but no worthy words to express it; she goes swimming, gets into the High Positive, and is astonished as the phrases come to her during a dive. The engineer has acres of discrete numbers on the left side but no formulas to express their relationships; while fly-fishing in the High Positive he catches a trout and the equations.

TRICKS OF THE TRADES

Creativity is both convergent and divergent, synthetic and analytic, right-brain and left-brain. It takes both sides to identify and solve problems. Some challenges lend themselves to one hemisphere, some to the other. When one approach doesn't work, try another.

But how do you go about switching dominant hemispheres on demand? When left-brain logic and analysis have boxed you in, how do you turn to the right-brain imagery and patterns? When the big picture is clear to you, but it's time to quantify it and put it into words and convey it to someone else, how do you get the left brain going? Wouldn't it be handy if there were a switch?

The switch is "handy"—right at hand, as it were.

If you normally do things with your right hand, and you want to fire up the right side of your brain, then use your left hand for a few minutes. Scribble, doodle, pick up small objects—any action that requires sustained concentration on muscular movement that is controlled by the right hemisphere. The electrical flow in your brain will change and the right side will become the more active.[6]

We have observed that many good performers do this automatically. When they're looking for ideas, they'll absent-mindedly doodle with their left hand; when they need to get those ideas into words, the switch occurs automatically as the pencil moves to the right hand.

Another technique along the same line is to plug your right nostril and breathe deeply through the left for about a minute. Recordings of the brain's electrical currents show that mental activity increases on the right side when your left nostril takes in most of your air. Normally, dominant hemispheres switch every ninety minutes or so anyway; the dominant nostril changes as the dominant hemisphere changes. But you don't have to wait.

Visual strategies can also change dominant hemispheres. If you need some right-brain activity, look at a picture—preferably quite abstract and meaningless, so that you won't be tempted to analyze it. Your eyes will move from left to right across the picture; your head will settle so that your left eye, which sends most of its information to the pattern-handling right hemisphere, does most of the work; and the right hemisphere will go to work. Conversely, if you need to examine something and then describe it in words, look at it with your right eye so that the information is processed in the verbal left hemisphere.

These simple physical strategies let you control which hemisphere dominates your thinking at a given time. This also explains why creative insights—that is, communication between the two problem-solving hemispheres—so often occur during physical activity. When the activity is involving but not exhausting, the brain is getting ample supplies of glucose and oxygen. Both hemispheres are active, since both sides of the body require coordination. The activity can be as simple as a brisk walk or as challenging as a 5.11 rock face—it stimulates both hemispheres and transforms problems into solutions.

APPLIED CREATIVITY

Deploying one hemisphere or the other is not a magic method; you won't solve all problems with a single right-brain synthesis or left-brain analysis. Given a math problem—say $x^3 - 2x^2 - 5x + 6$—you could try an analytic approach and factor with the integral terms. Or you could come in from the right side and graph the function. Either method will produce the roots $(1, -2, 3)$—if you know how to look at mathematical problems. If you don't know the techniques, it doesn't matter how many cerebral hemispheres you use.

The techniques for examining and solving mathematical problems have been codified; that's what you learn in algebra and geometry classes. Unfortunately, most formal education goes little further in explaining how to identify problems and search for solutions. That might explain why MBAs from Harvard, whose business school focuses on identifying and solving problems, are so sought after.[7]

Finding a solution generally means looking at a problem in a new way, from a different perspective. After all, if the conventional approaches worked, there wouldn't be a problem.

Remember that there are two facets to problem-solving, or indeed any creative act. One is generating ideas, and the other is evaluating those ideas. Don't try to do both at the same time when you're looking for answers. When the ideas are flowing, just note them and keep going; this isn't the time to be practical. When you evaluate the possible approaches or solutions, then call in the other creative skills—analysis, visualization, etc.

There are many techniques you can use to enhance creativity. For example:

Think Backward. Envision the desired result, and then figure out how to reach it. In formal terms, this is "end-use analysis." Adam Osborne revolutionized the computer industry in 1981 by thinking backward. The other manufacturers had focused on what they could build with the technology; Osborne thought of what people bought computers to do, and worked backward from there to produce a machine that would do those jobs. His company was soon shipping thousands of the ungainly but productive little machines every month. (One creative stroke isn't enough in a volatile industry, it must be noted.)[8]

Amid the warnings of doom and gloom concerning energy supplies in the early 1970s, physicist Amory Lovins looked backward. Instead of asking, "How do we develop more energy?" he asked, "How are we using the energy?" By examining it from that end, he realized that it was the use of energy, not its source, that was important to the American economy. His work was controversial, but in the end it led to major changes in American energy policy.[9]

Challenge Assumptions. Assumptions are not evil or unproductive. You'd never get through the day if you couldn't assume anything and felt compelled to check everything—spending an hour or two under the hood of your car before you started it, and then conducting some exhaustive chemical tests every time you filled the tank to be sure that the liquid was indeed gasoline. You'd have to ask for identification from everyone you met because you couldn't assume that they were giving you their proper names and affiliations. You'd look up every telephone number instead of assuming that you could remember correct numbers and assuming that the numbers hadn't been changed overnight.

But when you get a wrong number, you challenge your assumptions. The assumptions are always a good place to start when creativity is needed.

One of our favorite examples concerns an apartment building in New York City. Its tenants feared to come home from work. They had to wait in the lobby for the elevators—a great many of the working tenants in the building were using them at the same time. As each tenant waited in the lobby for the elevator, so did muggers and purse-snatchers. The owners of the building wanted to solve the problem, but it was going to cost a small fortune to rip out part of the building and install more elevators so that the tenants didn't have to wait so long to get to their apartments.

Marshall McLuhan, one of the great creative minds of the century, became aware of the problem. However, he challenged the assumption that the problem had to be solved with more elevators. If everyone didn't want to use the elevators at the same time, then the elevators were up to the task. The owners took his advice and devoted part of the lobby to a cocktail lounge, staffed by off-duty policemen. Some tenants, upon arrival, still went straight to their apartments. But most stopped in for a drink and a chance to socialize with their neighbors. With a crowd in the lobby every evening, the muggers went elsewhere. Because some people stopped for only one drink, and others tarried much longer, the flow of people in and out of the elevators was evened out—no more five o'clock rush. And the bar made money.[10]

Break It Up. Look at one small segment of the problem and follow it from there—it gives you a place to start.

Robert Pirsig used this approach, explained eloquently in *Zen and the Art of Motorcycle Maintenance*, when he taught college English in Montana.[11] Given anything in the entire universe for an essay topic, one student couldn't think of what to write about. But when he told her to start with the upper left brick on the front of the old opera house, the ideas and words started to pour.

If you've got a problem and you're stuck, find a piece of it and focus on that; often it will lead you to the solution. Or it may lead to something entirely new. Henri Becquerel, a French professor of physics, in 1895 found that a photographic plate that shouldn't have been exposed had an image on it. He first assumed that it had somehow been unwrapped, and if he'd stopped there, he'd have just thrown it into the trash and resolved to be more careful. But he challenged that assumption because the image was different from anything he had seen before. He focused on what might have created that image, and discovered radioactive energy, something that no physicist had suspected.[12]

Break Yourself Up. That is, break yourself up with laughter. The essence of humor is making unexpected connections. That is also the basis of creativity—making new connections. Making humor out of what is before you not only energizes you and improves your mood, but it starts the mental processes of creativity. Keep making jokes out of it, and eventually something will be worth taking seriously.

Make Analogies. What does it look like? What does it act like? What does it remind you of?

For instance, one of the potential customers in your territory will gladly schedule an appointment with you, but that's as far as it ever gets. He won't move. It's like trying to do business with a rock.

But don't stop at that. When you have to deal with a rock, how do you get it to respond? If it's real big, you could tunnel through it—so maybe you could get past this unresponsive client and deal with someone else in that organization. Explosives work on rocks—you don't want to dynamite a customer, but a dynamic and explosive presentation might do the job. All rocks succumb to erosion; perhaps you can wear him down. You can dodge a rock if it's in your way—and maybe you're letting this "rock" get in your way, and you'd be better off to leave it there, go around it, and focus on other customers.

Keep Probing. It would be hard to think of an invention that has changed modern life in more ways than the transistor—which, of course, was discovered by accident. The three-man team at Bell Laboratories was investigating the surface properties of germanium in 1947; when the researchers found the predicted patterns of electrical conductivity, they could have stopped. They had, after all, done their job.[13]

But they kept at it. Like the five-year-old who's always asking why and won't give up until satisfied, they continued to poke at the germanium, running current through the crystal instead of just along its surface. And then they found that a piece of rock could amplify electrical impulses.

Curiosity is a childish trait; childhood is when people are busiest at learning and solving problems. Refusing to settle for the obvious or superficial is essential to top performance.

CREATIVE ENVIRONMENTS

In many respects, creativity is like sex or communication or a host of other human desires—there isn't any sure way to encourage it or insure it, but there sure are a lot of ways to discourage it.

Ironically, one of the tools that was supposed to enhance creativity often works against it—the brainstorm.

Its concept is simple. Get a bunch of people in a room, have them say whatever comes to mind concerning a problem, and in twenty minutes, you'll have dozens of possible solutions.

In practice, though, it is seldom very productive of new

ideas or insights—one not-very-creative person working alone can generally come up with more ideas than result from a session with a dozen creative wizards.

Why? Certain group dynamics take over in those sessions. One person wisecracks all the way through in order to be entertaining. Another, angry at a colleague over some past slight, mocks every one of his suggestions, and soon the suggestions quit coming. Expressing unfettered ideas makes most people feel vulnerable and exposed; they quickly learn to protect themselves by either keeping quiet or trying to think of something impressive or acceptable, instead of just throwing out ideas.

The most important element of a creative environment, researchers have found, is the suspension of judgment during the generation of ideas. Don't use phrases like "That's great, but what would it cost?" or "We tried that once," or "You're missing a vital point."

Just collect the ideas; you can evaluate them later. Don't judge your own; just get them down.

THE LONELY ROAD

As necessary as creativity is, it does not lead one down the safe and comfortable path. It isn't "normal" to adopt a creative outlook, to see problems as challenges—but remember that winning isn't normal either. Most players lose.

Creative people aren't crazy. Although there have certainly been lunatic inventors and madman poets, no study has ever found a higher percentage of mental disturbance in creative people.[14]

But people aren't always easy to work with when they're being creative. Creativity is generally a solitary process which often keeps one from paying attention to the social factors that smooth everyday relationships, and other people can be a destructive annoyance when you're generating or evaluating ideas. Solitude and daydreaming, neither of which generally impresses a supervisor favorably, are almost integral to creativity.

The route to creativity means questioning assumptions and looking for problems—that is, rocking the boat, which is a ticket to trouble in some organizations.

And creativity takes energy. Not just to get an idea, but to carry it through adversity. No one will work as hard for your idea as you will.

Besides teaching people how to use their creativity, George M. Prince once invented for hire; he encountered the same result time and time again. "A client would pay us to invent something. We would do it. It would then languish with little or no further action.

"In contrast, the groups we worked with who did their own inventing would overcome one monstrous difficulty after another until they had a marketable product. The lesson gradually came clear to me: to change anything, to learn anything, to turn an idea into a product demands enormous energy and commitment."[15]

SMOOTHING THE LONG AND HARD ROAD

Enormous energy and commitment, the ready willingness to carry on through persistent adversity and frustration, the stamina to continue, the dedication to excellence—those are the hallmarks of top performers, the qualities of successful entrepreneurs, the results of applying the strategies of mental toughness to consistently perform in the High Positive regardless of external circumstances.

As George Gilder explains, "The most striking and paradoxical fact about the careers of successful entrepreneurs is their continual failure and frustration. . . . At the root and origin of all great empires of industry can usually be found a perspiring entrepreneur, often frustrated and fatigued, struggling over a machine that won't quite work."[16]

Henry Ford lost out at three auto companies and was

told, by the executives of the dominant auto firms at the time, that building a car that the masses could afford was impossible. J. R. Simplot agreed to deliver 500,000 pounds of onion flakes without owning any onion-processing machinery, or indeed any idea how it might be done. Armando Codina, an orphaned Cuban refugee, working days in a bank as a loan officer and nights in a doctor's office, devised a profitable way to computerize a blizzard of paperwork.

One of the most interesting entrepreneurs is Soichiro Honda.

Honda had but eight years of schooling; before World War II, he dedicated himself to casting piston rings. It came to the point that he had to move into the factory; his savings were exhausted and his wife had run out of jewelry to pawn. His first big order, fifty thousand units to Toyota, fell through because he couldn't meet the quality standards. He got up to Toyota's standards, but then couldn't expand his plant to meet the demand because the war had started and the Imperial Japanese government refused him rights to purchase cement. So he and his men learned how to make their own.

He lost two factories to fire-bombing, but rushed out after each raid to pick up the extra gasoline tanks that American pilots dropped. The tanks, Honda had found, contained metals he needed for his piston-ring alloys. After the war, he sold the piston-ring plant for $125,000 and started to build a new weaving machine for the textile industry. He ran out of money before he could manufacture it, and his car wouldn't take him anywhere that he might find food for his family because gasoline was severely rationed.

Soichiro Honda attached a motor to a bicycle; his neighbors were so impressed that they asked him to make more. The enterprise flourished until he ran out of surplus motors. The government still rationed gasoline and restricted the manufacture of gasoline-using engines. Honda built an engine that appeared to run on the resin squeezed from the roots of pine trees; generally, the idea was to mix a bit of resin with some black-market gasoline so that the entire mixture would reek of turpentine and convince suspicious authorities that the motorcycle was running on unrationed pine resin instead of illegal gasoline.

Thus began the world's largest motorcycle company. Years later, the emperor of Japan honored Honda for his contributions to restoring the economy of a nation devastated by war.

After the ceremony, the emperor's younger brother remarked, "It must be a very exacting task to invent or contrive something new."

Soichiro Honda, the man who had arrived at the imperial palace by living in a factory, pawning the family jewelry, scrounging for the leavings of the bombers that were destroying his factories, and enduring privations and setbacks, replied, "I don't really find it very exacting because I am doing what I like to do. As the proverb goes, 'Love shortens distances.' "

12

THE MYTH OF STRESS:
Cruising in the Fast Lane

IDEAL PERFORMANCE STATE: MOOD CONTROL

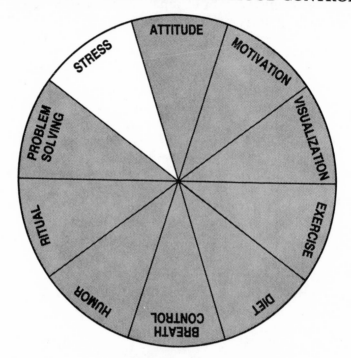

STRATEGIES

The harmful effects of stress are not caused by external events, but by your internal response to those events.

Control your internal response, and you can avoid the harmful effects of stress while continuing to perform in stressful environments.

The strategies of mental toughness allow you to control your internal response, and thus prevent the harmful effects of stress, in the face of seemingly overwhelming external events.

Only international terrorism and the national deficit receive more bad publicity than stress. Stress has been blamed for headaches, exhaustion, sexual dysfunction, asthma, ulcers, alcoholism, diabetes, diarrhea, drug addiction, insomnia, constipation, high blood pressure, strokes, heart disease, and most premature deaths from heart attacks. These stress-related disorders, in the view of Dr. Ronald Nathan at the University of Louisiana School of Medicine, afflict half of all Americans. Some experts hold that stress accounts for three-quarters of all visits to physicians. The National Safety Council estimates that 90 percent of all worker-compensation claims are based, ultimately, on stress.[1]

In the traditional view, stress is something that results from external events. While responding to continued stressful events, the mind and body eventually falter; the result is anything from a headache to a heart attack.

The emerging truth, however, points inward. Whether an external event is stressful or not is not determined by the event itself, but by your emotional response to the event. If you respond with fear or anger, then you succumb to stress, which will take its toll on your body and mind.

Managing stress does not mean managing your life so that you avoid change and challenge. It means controlling your emotional response to change and challenge so that you do not succumb to fear and anger. The strategies of emotional control—humor, motivation, attitude, exercise, diet, breath control, visualization—give you the tools to control your emotional responses.

STRESS IS THE RESPONSE, NOT THE EVENT

Top performers, in sports or business, respond differently to events that hold the potential to produce internal stress because they exercise better control of their Internal Energy States.

Each Internal Energy State has a characteristic response to potential stress. The state that you are in as you respond to an event determines whether the event is stressful or not.

HOW STRESS KILLS

The High Negative Internal Energy State is the familiar "fight or flight" response, and the Low Negative is fear in manifestations that range from immediate fright to omnipresent and looming dread and paranoia.

When you perceive something as a threat, the cognitive centers in your brain send a message to the hypothalamus, a gland in the limbic system, the seat of emotion. The hypothalamus releases the hormone ACTH into the bloodstream, which quickly reaches the adrenal cortex atop the kidneys. The adrenal cortex releases into the bloodstream certain other chemicals: epinephrine, norepinephrine, and the glucocorticoids.[2]

Epinephrine and norepinephrine (also known as adrenaline and noradrenaline) are closely related both chemically and in their effects on body and mind. They cause the sympathetic portion of the autonomic nervous system to take over from the parasympathetic—digestion slows, breathing becomes more rapid, the pupils dilate, blood clots more quickly, heartbeat quickens, blood pressure rises.

They differ, however, in that norepinephrine is more closely tied to anger and epinephrine to fear. If norepinephrine dominates, then the big muscles of the body are energized for a battle or for running away from the scene as rapidly as possible. When epinephrine dominates, the result is close to paralysis; the body is frozen in fear. The difference is most apparent in the face, which flushes with anger but pales in fear. Although the findings are not yet conclusive, there is good evidence that norepinephrine dominates this chemical response in men and epinephrine in women.[3]

In either case, the normal metabolism of the body is disrupted and long-term health suffers, especially if these responses occur frequently. High blood pressure becomes

INTERNAL ENERGY STATES
AND RESPONSE TO
POTENTIALLY STRESSFUL EVENTS

High Intensity

<u>**HIGH POSITIVE**</u>
Energy without tension

The Challenge Response

> "I can handle this. It is worth my time and effort. I enjoy solving problems and I will find a way to solve this problem. If my first effort does not work, I will stay at it until I find something that does work."

<u>**HIGH NEGATIVE**</u>
Tension with energy

The Anger Response

> "Why should I be dealing with something so stupid? This is really a joke. They're out to get me with this. I'll make sure they pay before all is said and done."

Pleasant ———————————————————— **Unpleasant**

<u>**LOW POSITIVE**</u>
Neither energy nor tension

The Avoid Response

> "This isn't worth worrying about. So I won't. I'll pay attention to what matters to me."

or

The Relax Response

> "I can't get out of this, so I'll find a way to enjoy it."

<u>**LOW NEGATIVE**</u>
Tension without energy

The Fear Response

> "I can't handle this. It's getting to me. It's going to destroy me. I don't know what to do."

Low Intensity

a way of life (and unfortunately death) instead of an occasional affliction. Glucocorticoids—the other chemicals released by the adrenal cortex—may account for most of the stress-related disease. Through several complicated chemical reactions, the glucocorticoids inhibit the workings of the body's immune system.[4]

There are reasons for this. Allergies, for example, are generally immune reactions. If you were threatened and trying to remain immobile and unnoticed, the last thing you'd want is to sneeze because of an allergy. If you were trying to run away or were engaged in battle with the threat, you wouldn't want to be gasping for breath at the same time because you had an attack of hay fever. This suppression of the immune system, in the face of a clear and immediate threat, saved our ancestors' lives.

But when there are repeated stress responses that damage the immune system, then the body lacks the tools it requires to fight disease. When fear and anger are the techniques for dealing with daily stress, then the immune system is never functioning properly. All those stress-related diseases gain a foothold and begin to work against the body whose defenses have been impaired.

Sustained negative emotions in response to stress can kill and maim directly by inducing high blood pressure and ulcers, and indirectly by encouraging the host of viruses and bacteria always trying to invade and conquer the human body. While there is always a possibility that those microbes will invade and cause trouble—there are many biological and environmental factors besides an improper response to stress that can lead to disease—staying on the positive side improves your overall health.

In short, a positive emotional outlook does not guarantee physical health, and disease has many causes other than responding to stressful events with fear or anger. But keeping yourself on the positive side is the best known way to put the odds on the side of your continued physical health and mental well-being.

WHAT, ME WORRY?

The Low Positive response to a potential source of stress is in a sense no response at all. It means staying comfortable and relaxed while refusing to respond to the event any more than is absolutely necessary. We want to emphasize that it is a perfectly valid way to deal with much of what life throws at you.

Suppose that you were counting on catching a certain flight, and the takeoff was delayed. The High Negative response—a consuming and rising anger at the morons who service the jets and the halfwits who pilot them and the numbskulls who sell tickets and the thousands of dimwits who own stock in such an ineptly run airline—won't change the external situation. You'll shorten your life span and the plane will still be late.

The results will be much the same with a Low Negative response. They knew it was important for you to be at your destination by a certain time. Just to sandbag you, four mechanics, a reservation clerk, and two controllers in the tower somehow conspired to ruin every chance you had of getting there on time. You start to worry about every catastrophe that might conceivably result from this delay —being late for the appointment will mean a missed opportunity that will lead to a career setback; your family and friends will give up on such a hopeless loser. The dread builds and you can feel your digestive tract contorting itself into exotic knots as yet undiscovered by sailors and Boy Scouts.

You fall into the If Only Syndrome: *If Only* you had not been so busy so that you could afford to waste half a day and arrange for an earlier flight, *If Only* you had made the appointment for another day, *If Only* that wasn't in your territory, *If Only* you had taken a different job six months ago when you had the opportunity, *If Only* you had stayed at your old job, *If Only* you had taken up another career, *If Only* you had not been born at all . . .

Responding with the Low Positive keeps you away from stress in such circumstances. You appraise the situation and realize that the delayed flight represents your only realistic way to get there—no other flights will serve as well, and you do not feel up to explaining how the charter of a Lear jet appeared on your expense account. You make the necessary telephone calls to explain the situation to those awaiting you, and forget about flying until it's time to board the plane. You did what you could, and now it's up to the airline.

The Low Positive is not a performance response. It is the best response when a performance isn't appropriate. If it's somebody else's headache, then let somebody else have the headache. Satisfy yourself that you have done what you can do with the situation, and ignore it. Not every situation demands a performance; use your energy when it will do some good.

BREAKING TRADITIONS

In the traditional view, stress is caused by external events that affect one's life. The events cause a stress reaction that leads to physical sickness, disability, and sometimes death.

You've certainly seen the charts and quizzes that rate stress: 94 points if someone close to you died during the past six months, 71 points for a divorce during the past year, 64 for a new job, 48 for an engagement, 19 for a mortgage, and so forth. You add up the total; if you beat 200 or some other arbitrary figure, then you are presumed likely to succumb to one or more of those stress-related afflictions in the near future. Get over 300 points, and you start to feel very fortunate to be alive at all.

Those charts and quizzes were the result of the first medical studies of stress; they performed a valuable service because they made it clear that stress and physical health are intimately linked.[5] Stress can make you nervous and tense and angry, or it can make you fearful and withdrawn and burned-out—in either case, your body suffers, and the consequences will range from headaches to heart attacks.

The problem with this view of stress was that it offered no realistic way to manage stress. Under this concept—that stress was something external—life gave you much the same bargain as the legendary Dr. John Faustus, the scholar of Wurtenburg, was offered by the demon Mephistopheles. Faustus was an ambitious man who had mastered law, medicine, and theology; he wanted more. Mephistopheles gave Faustus two options:

1. Abandon his ambitions and live out his allotted years in a serene and unchallenging routine.
2. Sell his soul, pursue his ambitions, but die in seven years.[6]

The modern stress version of this infernal dilemma went this way:

1. Avoid all potential sources of stress—that is, all challenges and changes—and you can be healthy and, if fortunate, long-lived.
2. Confront a life full of change and challenge. Such a life will almost certainly be short, brutish, and nasty, though, because all that stress will exact its toll on mind and body.

On its surface, that isn't much of a bargain, but it at least offered one way to escape the ravages of stress—just avoid any event that might produce stress.

But in fact there is no reasonable hope of beating stress if this traditional view is valid.

For one thing, some sources of stress are virtually unavoidable—the death or serious illness of a family member, loss of employment occasioned by a changing national economy, a close friend moving away.

For another, the same events that can produce all those dire consequences of stress—marriage, a promotion to a position of greater responsibility, a change in career—also bring joy and fulfillment to many people.

And finally, various studies demonstrated that just about

anything could produce stress. It wasn't just major life changes that generated stress. Minor events like telephones ringing at inconvenient times or missing a favorite television program were also shown to cause stress reactions.

Stress, it became clear, is woven into the fabric of life. It cannot be avoided if you are alive, and a full life means a life beset by onslaught after onslaught of potential stress.

Some people appeared to handle stress better than others, though, and researchers pressed to find out why. Was it because they were in superior physical condition—that is, they suffered as much as anyone else, but it just took more stress to overcome their physical systems and make them sick? Or was it because they had developed external support networks—family and friends—to support and comfort them? Or was it something else entirely that enabled top performers to avoid the debilitating effects of stress while continuing to perform superbly?

THE EMERGING TRUTH

The first indications came from Dr. Ray Rosenman and Dr. Meyer Friedman, who studied 3,154 healthy men in ten California corporations, looking into the roots of stress-induced heart disease. They found that the previous theories about the causes of heart disease had missed something important. Smoking, drinking, poor diet, excess weight, and lack of exercise all contributed to some degree to the likelihood of early heart attack, but the most significant factor had been missed in all previous studies. The leading cause of stress-induced heart attacks was a consistent pattern of being angry, impatient, and highly competitive, even in inconsequential matters. Men who lived that way, no matter how excellent their physical condition, were twice as likely to succumb to early heart attacks as the men who were unhurried, relaxed, and fulfilled in their daily lives.

Rosenman and Friedman's book, *Type A Behavior and Your Heart*, enriched the American vocabulary with Type

A and Type B personalities. But their analysis, brilliant as it was, lent itself to misinterpretation. The only hope for Type As, always impatient and angry, was to transform themselves into mellow Type Bs. Rosenman and Friedman emphasized that there were many successful Type Bs, and that Type A behavior was not a necessary component of success. Their point was valid, but when they looked for groups of Type Bs to study, they found municipal clerks and embalmers.

Thus many people continued to view stress and life as an extension of the infernal dilemma: Be a successful Type A, live in the fast lane, and run a tremendous risk of early death or disability, or be a run-of-the-mill Type B, living stresslessly and healthfully, but relinquishing ambition and achievement.

Rosenman and Friedman's work, however, pointed the way for Margaret Chesney, director of the Department of Behavioral Medicine at SRI International, the well-known California think tank. Teaming with Rosenman, she examined each component of Type A behavior—the obsession with time, the constant muscle tension, the continual competitiveness, and so forth—to find which one was most likely to produce heart disease. The answer was anger.

Chesney's findings show that the people who are most likely to suffer from stress are those who take every untoward event as a personal affront that makes them angry. If they have not developed ways to avoid or release that anger, then it builds and manifests itself as chronic high blood pressure leading to heart disease.[7]

THE HARDY EXECUTIVES

In the Midwest, Salvatore R. Maddi, professor in the Department of Behavioral Sciences at the University of Chicago, and Suzanne C. Kobasa, now associate professor of psychology at City University of New York, spent eight years studying stress among executives and managers at

Illinois Bell Telephone. Their work demolished the traditional view of stress.[8]

Maddi and Kobasa found that stressful events—the death
of a spouse, transfer, promotion, being passed over for
promotion, restructuring an always-regulated enterprise
to deal with emerging competition—can lead to long-term
health problems. But not in everyone. When they checked
the familiar stress tests and questionnaires, they discovered
they were only about 15 percent more accurate than flip-
ping a coin for predicting whether someone would suffer
from stress-related disease.

Overall physical well-being, they discovered, is of some
help in fighting stress. But they found executives in poor
physical condition who did not suffer from stress-related
afflictions, as well as executives who exercised hard and
frequently but also suffered from stress. A close and sup-
portive network of family and friends also helped, they
found. But again, there were too many exceptions for social support to explain why some executives handled stress
well and some did not.

Maddi and Kobasa found that the executives who best
handled stress—people who could keep themselves together and continue to perform at the upper end of their
abilities through transfer, divorce, death in the family, promotion, reassignment; people who carried a zest for life
—were those "hardy" executives who shared three qualities
lacking in the stressed executives who ended up with stress-
related health problems:

1. Commitment, instead of alienation. The hardy executives were interested in whatever they were doing and
   involved themselves in it. Seldom were they at a loss
   for something to do. In contrast, the stressed executives
   were often at a loss for leisure activities; they found
   their jobs boring and meaningless, and they resisted
   involvement.
2. Control, instead of powerlessness. The hardy executives
   believed and acted as if they could influence the events
   around them; they did not take things at face value and

they reflected on how to turn situations to their own advantage. The stressed executives felt that they were passive victims of forces beyond their control; they did not develop options and showed little initiative.

3. Challenge, instead of threat. The hardy executives considered change as something natural, and saw the changes as a stimulus to performance. To them, life may have been demanding, but it was also interesting and challenging. The stressed executives believed that stability was natural, and that any change had to be for the worse. Since they felt powerless, they were sure that change would necessarily disrupt whatever comfort and security they had managed to amass.

STRESS MANAGEMENT

Commitment, control, and challenge—if you can exercise those, you can beat stress and stress-induced illness. Consider Norman Cousins's laugh-therapy recovery from a disease believed incurable. Cousins was committed to returning to a productive life; he has always been fully involved in whatever he was doing. Cousins maintained a sense of control: He believed that he, through his attitudes and actions, could influence the course of a disease, and he did not feel powerless and unable to respond to this overwhelming change. Cousins saw a demanding challenge in the disease, even though everyone else saw a deadly threat.

Humor is only one of the strategies of mental toughness. The commitment, control, and challenge required to beat stress can also result from using other strategies. You cannot always control external situations. However, you can always control your emotional response to external events. Since stress is produced by the response, not the event, controlling your response is the same as eliminating stress.

Let's examine some events that typically cause stress, short-term or long-term, and see how our strategies provide the commitment, control, and challenge required to beat stress.

The Haunting Spectacle

You are driving to work one morning along a two-lane road. An oncoming car swerves out of its lane and collides head-on with the car immediately in front of you. Flying glass, twisted metal, blood, gashes, gritting pain, severe injuries: After you do what you can at the scene and then proceed to work, you can't put the sight out of your mind. Also, you cannot keep from telling yourself that, but for a quirk of fate, it could have been you.

If you could, you'd take the day off. But there are tasks you must perform today. Every time you try to focus on your work, though, those dreadful images return along with that chilling realization that you could just as easily have been among the victims. The more you try to focus on your work, the more intensely you relive the accident, and the more tense and anxious you feel about not getting your work done.

You're in no condition to perform, yet you know you must. The stress continues to mount.

You stop for a moment and realize that you're in the Low Negative because of mental imagery. So you deploy the visualization skills you have developed, first to relax, and then to energize. You're ready to perform.

With time, the horrifying images would have lost their power and would have been replaced with other, more positive, images. Visualization speeds up the process so that you can be at your best when you need to be.

Passed Over

You're barely able to walk as you leave a superior's office; someone else got the promotion you thought was coming to you, and you feel as though you were kicked in the stomach. You come up with an instant mental list of people you wish to spindle, fold, and mutilate.

When you're this tense, it's impossible for you to think clearly, so first you perform several enhanced shrugs to release the tension and anger.

Then you examine your motivation and realize why you

were passed over for promotion. You had wanted the promotion so much that you had been performing in the High Negative—you were focused on the outcome instead of the performance. No wonder the company wasn't impressed with your recent performance; it wasn't you at your best.

Your attitude didn't help, either. Because you wanted everything to look good so that you could get that promotion, you were avoiding change, instead of responding to it. Your attitude, when you examine it more closely, was that any changes were going to work against you; again, you were pushing yourself onto the negative side.

It's time to take stock, you tell yourself, so you do. You might conclude that nothing in your current assignment appeals to you and the only reason you stayed at it was in the hope of promotion. In that case, you have no commitment, and you're going to suffer from stress if you try to stay. So you look for something else that you believe is deserving of your commitment.

More likely, you will start looking for challenges at your current level—things that could be improved with your effort and involvement. With the commitment and challenge provided by this deployment of mental toughness, the stress vanishes. Your focus changes; when promotion time comes around again, you are almost reluctant to move up because you are so enjoying your current position.

In either case, you have used the most essential strategy of mental toughness: Focus on the controllable. You couldn't control the company's promotions, but you could control your own attitude and motivation, and thus you avoided the dire effects of stress.

Stage Fright

It's looming over you like a thunderhead. You must make an important presentation next week. If you blow it, you can say good-bye to your career, or at least to any hope of advancing in your career. It pervades every waking moment and it prevents you from sleeping soundly; you're running on nerves and you know that if this keeps up, you'll be a wreck by the time you must perform.

This performance is so important to you that you'll try anything to make sure you do well.

You find that regular exercise, after work each night, eases the tension immediately. It clears your mind of the office worries, you fall to sleep quickly at night, and you find more energy for your work.

You still feel that dread knotting up inside you, but you "catastrophize." You envision the worst that could happen as a direct result of totally punting your presentation. As nearly as you can tell, you'd keep your current job, which you like; you'd just be embarrassed for a while. You've been embarrassed before and you lived through it. The sun still came up in the east on the next morning. There's no consequence of failure that you can't handle.

Then you indulge in some mental rehearsal as you prepare. You also practice breath control to make your jitters vanish. You continue to focus on the controllable. You can't control the outcome of your presentation, but you can, through your efforts, insure that it is an intelligent and coherent presentation, coming from someone who is confident and competent. The upcoming performance ceases to be a threat to your well-being and becomes instead a challenge; meeting it will require every skill you can muster, but you know you have whatever it will take. As you exercise and visualize, the stress departs from your life.

You'd never have believed it was possible, but quickly you begin to enjoy those demanding presentations—which is good, because with the big promotion you received after your first presentation went over so well, you're making a lot of them.

Waiting in Line

It doesn't have to be a literal line, of course. It might just be that you've got to get in touch with someone and her secretary tells you that there's no chance before four o'clock—but you've got to put her information into a report that's due at five o'clock and will take at least two hours to put together. Or perhaps it's a traffic jam when you've got to be somewhere five minutes ago.

Wishing that the clock would move slower, or the line in front of you would move faster, is one of the most certain ways to find yourself physically impaired by stress.

Use the first strategy of emotional control and examine your own Internal Energy State during these impatient situations. Does having to wait for something put you into the High Negative by making you anxious and angry? Or does it put you into the Low Negative by making you feel withdrawn and powerless?

Breath control and quick exercises provide rapid relief for physical and mental tension. The next step is to decide what you want to do with the time. As we pointed out earlier, it is just as important to know how to relax as how to perform. So take the time to relax, perhaps by using visualization. And the stress will disappear.

Or energize and turn your focus to something you can control. While you're waiting for someone to call, you could be meeting another challenge, instead of fretting and stewing. Pay attention to what you can do now, instead of worrying about what you can't do. This ability to shift your focus gives you a powerful mechanism for managing stress.

Life is full of unavoidable delays. If you can do something about them, then do something about them. If they're out of your control, then pay attention to what you can control. Those unavoidable delays are really opportunities—opportunities to relax, or opportunities to perform well at something else.

Death

The death of a spouse or someone close to you offers more potential for damaging stress than any other event you will experience.[9] Grief and an overwhelming sense of loss are totally natural at such times. It is not natural that a survivor's health or long-term ability to perform should be permanently damaged by grief, yet that is too often the outcome. When one partner in a marriage dies, the other's life expectancy drops precipitously.

In such overwhelming circumstances, do not try to perform. You will be on the Negative side for some time, and any time you energize yourself to perform, you'll find yourself in the High Negative.

Focus on what you can control. You cannot bring back someone you cared for. But you can keep yourself from falling apart physically by maintaining your diet, exercise, and regular sleep habits. You can substitute positive images of the good times (after all, how would you prefer to be remembered?) for any negative imagery that bothers you. Life may seem hollow and meaningless, and your long-term motivation may be nonexistent; shift to an immediate focus, getting the best you can out of each minute.

A period of mourning and withdrawal is natural. You have lost an important part of your life; recovery and re-growth require time. It is within your power to insure that this time is an interval of healing and growth, rather than a reign of anxiety and alienation.

LONG-TERM STRESS

Nothing produces more damaging stress than struggling through a life that is inconsistent with your own goals and ideals. Exercise, diet, visualization, humor, and the other strategies of emotional control will mitigate the momentary stresses, but there is no strategy that will keep you from suffering from long-term stress if your life is incompatible with your beliefs.

Consider the polygraph—the lie detector. All it really measures is the physical response to stress—elevated pulse, quickened respiration, changed skin chemistry reflected in its electrical conductivity, etc. If the few seconds that it takes to tell a lie can cause all those adverse physical stress reactions, then how much more must your body suffer if you attempt to live a lie?

Fortunately, it is always within your power to change.

Afterword

So long as you aspire and achieve, practice and perform, there will remain a gap between what you want to be and what you are, a world of frustrations and annoyances that beset you as you seek sustained excellence.

The journey is not an easy one, and it will never end.

The key is to enjoy the trip.

When you're at your best, in your Ideal Performance State, there is no difference between what you want to be doing and what you actually are doing. You are totally focused on meeting the challenge of the moment. Aware and confident, energized yet relaxed, you exult in the battle. You cannot control the outcome, but you are in full mastery of what you can control—your attitudes and skills. You are doing precisely what you want to do, what gives you satisfaction and joy.

The Ideal Performance State has been most studied in athletes, but it belongs to everyone who pursues quality with a passionate intensity. It has been yours during those "white moments" that you remember so clearly, moments that will come with increasing frequency.

Performing well is a result of feeling good, of being in the right emotional state. Your emotional state is not some uncontrollable mystery, but the reflection of the chemistry of your nervous system.

We have given you the most accessible and most powerful of the many tools you can use to maintain and enhance that control while filling your reservoirs of personal energy. With the strategies of mental toughness, you have the power to narrow the gap between what you are and what you want to be.

No matter how long or arduous your journey, you will enjoy every step.

Recommended Reading

GENERAL

No one explains the complexities of science more clearly than Isaac Asimov. *Isaac Asimov on the Human Body and the Human Brain* (New York: Bonanza Books, 1984) is lucid and easy to understand. It is, however, somewhat dated, since this is a one-volume reprint of two works originally published in 1963.

For an overview of the human mental processes, read *The Brain: The Last Frontier* (New York: Warner Books, 1979), by Richard M. Restak, M.D.

CHAPTER ONE

This book grew out of *Athletic Excellence: Mental Toughness in Sports* (Denver: Forum, 1982), by Dr. James E. Loehr, which goes into more detail concerning sports and coaching situations. Reissued as *Mental Toughness Training in Sports* (Lexington, Mass.: Stephen Greene Press, 1986).

The C Zone (Garden City, N.Y.: Anchor Press/Doubleday, 1984), by Robert Kriegel and Marilyn Harris Kriegel, focuses on the same topic as this book; we'd be hard-pressed to define the difference between the C Zone and the Ideal Performance State. However, we identify it as a distinct emotional state and offer specific strategies of emotional control in order to reach that state.

Another book with a similar theme is *Peak Performance* (Los Angeles: Jeremy P. Tarcher, 1984), by Charles A. Garfield with Hal Zina Bennett. He stresses athletic performance; we look at all arenas.

CHAPTER TWO

Although it is quite technical, *The Psychology of Fear and Stress* (New York: McGraw-Hill, 1971), by Jeffrey Gray, offers valuable background information.

The best overall view of psychobiology is found in *The Psychobiology of Mind* (Hillsdale, N.J.: Lawrence Erlbaum Associates, 1978), by William R. Uttal. But don't expect it to be easy reading.

CHAPTER FIVE

The power of visualization is detailed in *Seeing with the Mind's Eye* (New York: Random House, 1975), by Mike Samuels and Nancy Samuels.

Landscapes of the Night: How and Why We Dream (New York: Viking, 1984), by Christopher Evans and edited by Peter Evans, is also well worth reading.

CHAPTER SIX

Although there are scores of exercise books, one of the earliest remains among the best—*Aerobics* (New York: M. Evans, 1967), by Dr. Kenneth Cooper.

CHAPTER SEVEN

The best single source of nutrition information we encountered is *The Nutrition Almanac* (New York: McGraw-Hill, 1984) edited by John D. Kirschmann.

CHAPTER EIGHT

Naturally, we recommend *Take a Deep Breath*, (New York: Villard, 1986), by James E. Loehr, Jeffrey Migdow, M.D., and Jerome Agel.

CHAPTER NINE

If you haven't read it already, do read *Anatomy of an Illness* (New York: Bantam, 1981) by Norman Cousins.

CHAPTER ELEVEN

The author's politics are sometimes hard to take, but the writing is consistently excellent and the accounts are fascinating in *The Spirit of Enterprise* (New York: Simon and Schuster, 1984), by George Gilder.

CHAPTER TWELVE

By all means, read *The Hardy Executive: Health Under Stress* (Homewood, Ill.: Dow Jones–Irwin, 1984), by Salvatore R. Maddi and Suzanne C. Kobasa.

Source Notes

CHAPTER ONE

1 Much of the early research is detailed in Dr. James E. Loehr's *Athletic Excellence: Mental Toughness in Sports* (Denver: Forum, 1982). Significant additional research which confirms his work appears in *The Evaluation of a Program for the Teaching of Essential Mental Skills in Sport*, by Charles Foster Glore, a doctoral thesis submitted in 1981 to the School of Education, University of Colorado.

2 Arnold Palmer, *Go for Broke* (New York: Simon and Schuster, 1973), 193.

3 Babe Ruth, as told to Bob Considine, *The Babe Ruth Story* (New York: Dutton, 1948), 193.

4 H. L. Mencken, "The Divine Afflatus," *A Mencken Chrestomathy* (New York: Random House Vintage, 1982), 442.

5 Robert Kriegel and Marilyn Harris Kriegel, *The C Zone* (Garden City, N.Y.: Anchor Press/Doubleday, 1984), 1.

6 Irving Dardik, M.D., F.A.C.S., and Dennis Waitley, Ph.D., *Breakthrough to Excellence: Quantum Fitness* (New York: Pocket Books, 1984), 47.

7 Kriegel and Kriegel, 2.

8 Edward de Bono, *Tactics: The Art and Science of Success* (Boston: Little, Brown and Co., 1984), 205.

9 Interview with workshop participant, March 13, 1985, Denver, Colo.

10 See any of the following:
Paul Hawken, *The Next Economy* (New York: Ballantine, 1983).
Rosabeth Moss Kanter, *The Change Masters: Innovation and Entrepreneurship in the American Corporation* (New York: Simon and Schuster Touchstone, 1983).
John Naisbitt, *Megatrends: Ten New Directions Transforming Our Lives* (New York: Warner Books, 1984).
Gifford Pinchot III, *Intrapreneuring* (New York: Harper & Row, 1984).
Louis Ruckeyser, *What's Ahead for the Economy* (New York: Simon and Schuster Touchstone, 1983).

11 Abraham H. Maslow, *Toward a Psychology of Being* (New York: Van Nostrand Reinhold, 1963), 71–102.

12 Isaac Asimov, *Isaac Asimov on the Human Body and the Human Brain* [Reprint in one volume of two books originally published separately in 1963.] (New York: Bonanza Books, 1984), 468.
13 Richard M. Restak, *The Brain: The Last Frontier* (New York: Warner Books, 1979), 132–136.
14 William R. Uttal, *The Psychobiology of Mind* (Hillsdale, N.J.: Lawrence Erlbaum Associates, 1978), 335–343.
15 Walter Shapiro and others, "Reagan Wins a Draw," *Newsweek* (Oct. 29, 1984): 26–29.
16 Loehr, 32–44.
17 Restak, 309.
18 Quoted in *The New York Times*, Nov. 24, 1963.

CHAPTER TWO

1 Wayne Coffey, *303 of the World's Worst Predictions* (New York: Tribeca Communications, 1983), 75.
2 Loehr, 57–58.
3 Jeffrey Gray, *The Psychology of Fear and Stress* (New York: McGraw-Hill, 1971), 61–65.
4 The Diagram Group, *The Brain: A User's Manual* (New York: Berkley, 1984), 404–425.
5 Asimov, 378.
6 Gray, 53–67.
7 George Leonard, "Margaret Chesney's Affair of the Heart," *Esquire* (Dec. 1984): 76.
8 Maya Pines, "Stress Tolerance Makes the Difference," *Psychology Today* (Dec. 1980): 34–36.
9 Carl Sagan, *The Dragons of Eden: Speculations on the Evolution of Human Intelligence* (New York: Ballantine, 1977), 55–64.
10 Sagan, 72–80.
11 Howard Gardner, *The Mind's New Science: A History of the Cognitive Revolution* (New York: Basic Books, 1985), 119–121.
12 The Diagram Group, 316.
13 Uttal, 339–340.
14 Gray, 55.
15 Asimov, 342, 554.
16 B. J. Plasket and Ed Quillen, *The White Stuff: The Bottom Line on Cocaine* (New York: Dell, 1985), 32.

CHAPTER THREE

1   De Bono, 145–155.
2   Lee Iacocca and William Novak, *Iacocca: An Autobiography* (New York: Bantam, 1984), 165.
3   C. T. Onions, editor, *The Oxford Dictionary of Etymology* (Oxford: Oxford University Press, 1966), 203. It is there stated that the "con" syllable is an intensifier, rather than the Latin for "with." Most other dictionaries at hand agree with "with faith."
4   Steven F. Maier and Mark Laudenslager, "Stress and Health: Exploring the Links," *Psychology Today* (Aug. 1985): 44–49.
5   This is from Dr. Loehr's work with Gullikson.
6   C. B. Palmer, "War for the POW's Mind," *The New York Times Magazine* (Sept. 13, 1953): 134.
7   Jerry Mander, *Four Arguments for the Elimination of Television* (New York: William Morrow, 1979), 83.
8   *Encyclopaedia Britannica*, 11th ed., vol. VI, p. 209.
9   Susan Szasz, "Smiles," *Parents* (July 1980): 56.
10 Paul Eckman, Robert W. Levenson, and Wallace V. Friesen, "Autonomic Nervous System Activity Distinguishes Among Emotions," *Science* (Sept. 16, 1983): 1208–1210.
11 "Making Marines," *Life* (Nov. 24, 1972): 74–83.
12 M. Wilhelm, "His wife and former followers question the human potential of est guru Werner Erhard," *People* (Sept. 24, 1984): 41–42.

CHAPTER FOUR

1   Bernard Shaw, "The King and the Doctors," A Prose Anthology, edited by H. J. Burton (New York: Fawcett, 1965), 165.
2   Maslow, 197.
3   Ecclesiastes 9:11.
4   Dr. Loehr's conversations with Connors.
5   De Bono, 53.
6   De Bono, 51.
7   De Bono, 54.
8   De Bono, 51–52.
9   Paul Freiberger and Michael Swaine, *Fire in the Valley: The Making of the Personal Computer* (Berkeley, Calif.: Osborne/McGraw-Hill, 1984), 97–126.

10 Stephen Wozniak, "Homebrew and How the Apple Came
    To Be," *Digital Deli* (New York: Workman Publishing, 1984),
    74.
11 From Chapter 2 of *The Adventures of Tom Sawyer.*
12 Maier and Laudenslager.
13 Donald R. Katz, "Guru of the New Economy," *Esquire* (Dec.
    1984): 302.
14 Dorothy V. Harris and Bette L. Harris, *An Athlete's Guide to
    Sports Psychology: Mental Skills for Physical People* (Champaign,
    Ill.: Leisure Press, 1983), 133–145.
15 Quoted in *Time* (Feb. 2, 1968):, 38.

CHAPTER FIVE

1 Sagan, 70–72.
2 Interview with workshop participant.
3 Interview with workshop participant.
4 Restak, 328.
5 Roger Shepard and Jacqueline Metzer, "Mental Rotation of
   Three-Dimensional Objects," *Science* 171:701–703.
6 Mike Samuels and Nancy Samuels, *Seeing with the Mind's Eye*
   (New York: Random House, 1975), 34.
7 Charles A. Garfield with Hal Zina Bennett, *Peak Performance: Mental Training Techniques of the World's Greatest Athletes* (Los Angeles: Jeremy P. Tarcher, 1984), 93.
8 Richard Suinn, "Body Thinking: Psychology for Olympic
   Champs," *Psychology Today* (July 1976).
9 Samuels and Samuels, 57.
10 Elmer Green and Alyce Green, *Beyond Biofeedback* (New York:
   Dial Press, 1977), 74–77.
11 *Rocky Mountain News* (Denver, Colo.), April 17, 1985.
12 Bureau of the Census, United States Department of Com-
   merce, *Statistical Abstract of the United States: 1984* (Washington: Government Printing Office, 1983), 783, 568–69.
13 Roger W. Sperry, "Lateral Specialization in the Surgically
   Separated Hemispheres," *The Neurosciences: Third Study Program* (Cambridge, Mass.: MIT Press, 1974), 5–19.
14 Christopher Evans, *Landscapes of the Night: How and Why We
   Dream* (New York: Viking, 1984).
15 *Invention of the Sewing Machine.* Singer Sewing Machine Co.,
   1955.

16   Ronald W. Clark, *Einstein: The Life and Times* (New York: Avon, 1971), 150–57.

17   F. C. Kelly, *The Wright Brothers* (New York: 1943), 61–64.

18   Jack Nicklaus, *Golf My Way* (New York: Simon & Schuster, 1974), 79.

19   Abraham Horst, "A New Way of Seeing," *Skiing* (Feb. 1983): 44.

20   Loehr, 128.

21   Claire Kopp, "Images of Flight," *Flying* (April 1985): 100–101.

22   David Wallechinsky, Irving Wallace, and Amy Wallace, *The Book of Lists* (New York: William Morrow and Company, 1977), 469.

23   Interview with workshop participant.

24   Interview with workshop participant.

25   He asked not to be named.

26   Neil Postman and Charles Weingartner, *Teaching as a Subversive Activity* (New York: Delta, 1969), 80.

CHAPTER SIX

1   Brad Darrach, "Chess Champion Bobby Fischer Is Deep in Training," *Life* (May 19, 1972): 84–88.

2   Asimov, 504.

3   Diane Hales and Robert Hales, "Using the Body to Mend the Mind," *American Health* (June 1985): 28.

4   Plasket and Quillen, 32.

5   Barbara Villet, "Opiates of the Mind: The Biggest Medical Discovery Since Penicillin," *Atlantic Monthly* (July 1979): 82–89.

6   Hales and Hales, also Ashley Grossman and John R. Sutton, "Endorphins: What are they? How are they measured? What is their role in exercise?" *Medicine and Science in Sports and Exercise*, Vol. 17, No. 1, pp. 74–81.

7   Observation of Loehr's during visit to Japan.

8   Asimov, 504.

9   Asimov, 236.

10   Ed Funk, "Avoiding Altitude Sickness," *Summit County Journal* (Breckenridge, Colo.) (Jan. 12, 1978): 7.

11   Carlton Fredericks, *New Low Blood Sugar and You* (New York: Putnam Perigee, 1985), 23.

12 Kenneth Cooper, *Aerobics* (New York: M. Evans, 1967), 87–92.
13 Asimov, 238.
14 A. C. Lesher, "The Canadian Idea: Fitness Should Be Fun," *SPORT* (March 1984): 14.
15 Gina Maranto, "Pain from the Sporting Life," *Discover* (Oct. 1984): 20.
16 Interview with Loehr.
17 Cooper, 37–53.
18 Julian Armstrong, "Fitness Regime Pays Healthy Dividends," *Gazette* (Montreal), (March 16, 1982).
19 Asimov, 102.

CHAPTER SEVEN

1 Asimov, 503.
2 Richard J. Wurtman, "The Ultimate Head Waiter: How the Brain Controls Diet," *Technology Review* (July 1984): 42ff.
3 Maya Pines, "What You Eat Can Affect Your Brain," *Reader's Digest* (Sept. 1983): 56.
4 John D. Kirschmann, editor, *The Nutrition Almanac* (New York: McGraw-Hill, 1984), 1.
5 Fredericks, 28.
6 Asimov, 366.
7 Stuart Berger, "Food Can Change Your Mood," *Parade* (Dec. 23, 1984): 12.
8 Asimov, 368.
9 Asimov, 236.
10 " 'Grazers' eat 5 or 6 times a day," *The Denver Post* (Aug. 4, 1985).
11 Kirschmann, 283.
12 Kirschmann, 90.
13 Kirschmann, 239–40.
14 Albert Creff and Robert Wernick, *The Maximum Performance Sports Diet* (New York: Kensington, 1979), 39–54.
15 Creff and Wernick may have been the first to suggest this method.
16 Judith Rodin and Elizabeth Hall, "A Sense of Control," *Psychology Today* (Dec. 1984): 42.

CHAPTER EIGHT

1   Asimov, 211.
2   Genesis 2:7.
3   Dina Ingber, "Brain Breathing," *Science Digest* (June 1981): 72ff.
4   Jacquelyn Wonder and Priscilla Donovan, *Whole Brain Thinking: Working from both sides of the brain to achieve peak job performance* (New York: Ballantine, 1985), 45.
5   "Breathing Cycle Linked to Hemispheric Dominance," *Brain/Mind Bulletin* (Jan. 3, 1983): 1.
6   Plasket and Quillen, 110–11.
7   James E. Loehr, Jeffrey A. Migdow, *Take a Deep Breath* (New York: Villard Books, 1986).
8   Asimov, 144.
9   Carl Stough with Reece Stough, *Dr. Breath: The Story of Breathing Coordination* (New York: William Morrow and Company, 1970).
10 Loehr, Migdow, and Agel.
11 Asimov, 149.
12 "Breathing Linked to Personality," *Psychology Today* (July 1983): 109.
13 Ingber.
14 "A Counterblast to Tobacco," 1604, *The Great Thoughts*, compiled by George Seldes (New York: Ballantine, 1985), 203.

CHAPTER NINE

1   Norman Cousins, *Anatomy of an Illness: Reflections on Healing and Regeneration* (New York: Bantam, 1981), 27–48.
2   Interview with Peter McLaughlin.
3   Carey McWilliams, *Ambrose Bierce: A Biography* (New York: Archon Books, 1967), 239–41.
4   De Bono, 168.
5   Hugh D. Menzies, "The Ten Toughest Bosses," *Fortune* (April 21, 1980): 65.
6   Harvey Mindess, *Laughter and Liberation* (Los Angeles: Nash Publishing, 1971).
7   Perry W. Buffington, "Make 'Em Laugh," *Sky* (April 1984): 58.
8   Jaclyn Fierman, "Fun in the Boredroom: Jim Henson has made a business of Muppet mini-movies that enliven meetings," *Fortune* (Feb. 4, 1985): 48–49.

9 Nancy Faber, "Bob Basso Believes You Can Laugh Your Troubles Away—And Big Business is Buying his Therapy," *People* (June 17, 1984).

10 Walter Kiechel III, "Executives Ought to be Funnier," *Fortune* (Dec. 12, 1983): 208.

11 "No Laughing Matter," *Time* (March 2, 1981): 71.

12 Max Eastman, *Reflections on the Failure of Socialism* (New York: 1926), 721.

13 William James, *The Principles of Psychology* (Boston: 1890), Vol. II, 118.

14 De Bono, 125–126.

15 Begley and Carey.

16 Kiechel.

17 Interview with Peter McLaughlin.

18 Ed Magnuson, "Oh My God, It's Happening," *Time* (April 13, 1981): 24.

19 Kiechel.

20 I've heard this one for years, and I sure can't nail it down anywhere.

21 Albert Rapp, *The Origins of Wit and Humor* (New York: E. P. Dutton, 1951), 143.

22 Dr. Donald W. Black, *Journal of the American Medical Association* (December 1984).

23 Wilfred Funk, *Word Origins* (New York: Bell Publishing, 1950), 16–17.

24 Antonia van der Meer, "So This Is Fitness?" *Health* (Jan. 1983): 19.

CHAPTER TEN

1 Judith Zimmer, "Courting the Gods of Sport," *Psychology Today* (July 1984): 36ff.

2 Louis S. Goodman and Alfred Z. Gilman, *The Pharmacological Basis of Therapeutics*, 4th edition, 1970.

3 Restak, 212.

4 Evans.

CHAPTER ELEVEN

1 Mencken.

2 B. Ghiselin, editor, *The Creative Process* (New York: Doubleday, 1966), 37.

3 Ghiselin, 41.

4   Philip J. Davis and Reuben Hersh, *The Mathematical Experience* (Boston: Houghton Mifflin, 1981), 169.
5   Restak, 187–232.
6   Wonder and Donovan, 117–123.
7   J. Melvon, "Harvard's Waffle Case," *Time* (May 4, 1981): 64.
8   Adam Osborne and John Dvorak, *Hypergrowth: The Rise and Fall of Osborne Computer Corporation* (Berkeley: Idthekkethan Publishing Co., 1984), 11.
9   Interview with Ed Quillen.
10 Interview with Peter McLaughlin.
11 Robert Pirsig, *Zen and the Art of Motorcycle Maintenance: An Inquiry into Values* (New York: Bantam, 1975), 171.
12 Robert Halisman, *The Story Behind Major Discoveries* (New York: Crown, 1972), 41.
13 Halisman, 116.
14 Martin Patterson, editor, *Readings in Creativity* (New York: McGraw-Hill, 1964), 371.
15 Patterson, 409.
16 George Gilder, *The Spirit of Enterprise* (New York: Simon and Schuster, 1984), 28–34, 98–108, 155–59, 178, 183.

CHAPTER TWELVE

1   Julian Weiss, "Stress: The Invisible Killer," *Gallery* (Feb. 1985): 44.
2   Gray, 53–67.
3   Weiss.
4   Asimov, 413.
5   Donald B. Ardell, "A Wellness Alternative to Managing Stress," *Optimal Health* (May/June 1985): 22.
6   In Christopher Marlowe's play, Faust gets twenty-four years instead of seven.
7   Leonard.
8   Salvatore R. Maddi and Suzanne C. Kobasa, *The Hardy Executive: Health Under Stress* (Homewood, Ill.: Dow Jones–Irwin, 1984).
9   Suzanne Oullette Kobasa, "How Much Stress Can You Survive?" *American Health* (Sept. 1984): 64–77.